the
SCREAM
of the
BUTTERFLY

the challenge of "substitute" parenting

the
SCREAM
of the
BUTTERFLY

the challenge of "substitute" parenting

Gary C. Barnett

Deeds Publishing
Marietta, Georgia

Published by Deeds Publishing
Marietta, GA
www.deedspublishing.com

Printed in the United States of America

Cover design by Mark Babcock

Library of Congress Cataloging-in-Publications Data is available upon request.

ISBN 978-1-937565-40-4

Books are available in quantity for promotional or premium use. For information, write Deeds Publishing, PO Box 682212, Marietta, GA 30068 or info@deedspublishing.com.

First Edition, 2012

10 9 8 7 6 5 4 3 2 1

"May the wings of the butterfly kiss the sun
And find your shoulder to light on.
To bring you luck, happiness, and riches
Today, tomorrow, and beyond."
- Irish blessing

Special thanks to…

The Hillcrest kids, their families, and my colleagues.

My children and their spouses, Jamie and Dave, Josh and Amy. To watch you all parent your children is one of my greatest pleasures.

My grandchildren –true joys and delights- Simon, Maya Rose, Leo, Bella Rae, Knox, Ozzie (we never got to hold you in our arms but we hold you in our hearts), and Moses (who is on the way!!)

Deeds Publishing—Jan, Bob, Mark, and crew. Your belief and support were tremendous. Maybe there is such a thing as serendipity!

Last but certainly first, Cindy… 45 years and counting. The best I am seems to be because of you… without you I am not me. Nothing makes me happier than to see you smile and make you laugh.

Contents

Introduction

"Before I sink into the big sleep, I want to hear, I want to hear...the Scream of the Butterfly."
- Jim Morrison, The Doors, When the Music's Over

"Fuck you, Motherfucker, you ain't my Momma and you ain't my Daddy, too!"

Timmy, with tears cutting dirt tracks down his scarred cheeks, was defiant, bewildered, and terrified, shouting all of his rage in my face as he held tightly to the front porch column.

I, along with a veteran caseworker, had just shown up at his home in the morning to take Timmy into custody and place him in out of home care in a residential treatment facility. He did not know me, and I knew him only by reputation. He and his siblings had been running amok in the community for most of the summer months following the death of their father. Timmy was supposedly the "hardcore" member of this sibling group and had been the leader in various juvenile offenses and scams in the neighborhood.

Timmy would knock on the front door of an unsuspecting neighbor while his younger sisters went through the back door to pilfer what they could find, money and food being their primary targets. Most of this behavior was driven by their need for food and sustenance as their mother had basically shut down, non-responsive and reclusive since the death of her husband. We, the local child welfare agency, were involved due to the ages of the children as Timmy was ten years old and his sisters eight and six. I had been working for about three months and had just been placed in the child welfare section of our agency... this was my first day in the "field," and I had inherited this family.

We were removing Timmy as his mother had repeatedly failed to provide the basic care for him and his siblings, and they were not attending school. The Juvenile Court had ruled that he was what would later be termed a CHINS (Child In Need of Services) rather than a delinquent. It was our hope that removing him and obtaining the necessary services might serve to motivate his mother into accepting services voluntarily for the other children.

Regardless of the court order, Timmy was not going with us without offering stiff resistance, wrapping himself around the column with his hands and legs. As I went to pry his fingers from the column he responded by biting me on the wrist. I was finally able to loosen his grip, obtain a hold and escort him to the car where my co-worker waited with the engine running. A casual observer unaware of the circumstances would have sworn Timmy was a "kidnap" victim more so than a child in need of services.

As I was lugging Timmy to the car and he shouted obscenities at the top of his voice, I must admit I was not thinking about his metamorphosis into a beautiful butterfly, although he screamed throughout the ordeal.

I worked with Timmy, his mother and two younger sisters over the next three years and got to know the family and their history very well.

Timmy's words spewed into my face had a special meaning for him and have stuck in my mind all of these years. He and his mother had witnessed his father's death in the streets, having seen him shot and left to die in the gutter. Timmy was left to stand guard over his dying father while his mother ran a few blocks to their home, woke the rest of the children and marched them back to see their father bleed to death.

I can only imagine that scene and the horror. I tried to keep that image fresh in my mind when engaged with these children. That emotional scar hurt Timmy more than the cut on his cheek that he received in a fight and it continued to reverberate throughout his life.

That particular encounter was my "professional" introduction to the world of children who are abused, neglected, runaways, and cast offs from their homes, as well as our communities.

When I think of Timmy I remember my Grandmother Meyer's admonition to me when I was starting off in this business, "Gary, we are too old too soon and too smart too late."

With Timmy I wish I had been smarter as I would have handled the situation in a different mode. I am sure my actions caused more trauma, although unintentional, and with the best concerns for him in my young mind. I know it took me more time to build a relationship of respect and eventual trust as I was an agent of trauma more so than a reliever of such.

Since that time I have tried to remind myself, "Gary, whatever you do, don't cause this youngster more pain!"

My "personal" introduction to such children as Timmy came years earlier when I was ten years old. That introduction has also stayed with me over the years and is as clear today as it was 50 years ago.

My father, a high school teacher and coach, worked summer months as a summer school teacher and recreational director at the same youth home where I was later to spend most of my career. It was the early 1960's and as was the case with most families, those that were fortunate to have an automobile had only one.

My mother had driven to the youth home to pick dad up from work after a long Friday that lasted into the early evening hours. She sent me through the front door to locate his office and let him know we were waiting.

As I came through the front door I entered a small waiting area that had a long church pew type bench against one wall across from the main office. I was startled to see a young girl, probably my age or younger, curled in a ball, fast asleep, using a battered old suitcase as her pillow. I located my father and as we were leaving I asked him and the superintendent of the home what was she doing there. All of the other children were either outside playing or finishing dinner chores. They told me that she had been there since shortly after lunch waiting on her parents to pick her up for a weekend visit. Her parents were to have arrived prior to lunch but had yet to show up or phone. The Superintendent explained that this happened quite often to many of the children in the facility.

This particular girl had steadfastly refused to leave the bench except to use the bathroom as she was afraid she would miss her folks. Throughout the day she insisted to any who inquired that they were coming for her and she did not want to miss them when they walked through the door. During dinner she apparently fell asleep. As we left I watched the superintendent gently pick her up and carry her back to her dorm area. I later found out her parents never did arrive or send word as to the reason for the missed visitation.

Unfortunately as the years have passed I have witnessed similar scenarios time and time again—not just with parents and relatives, but other people who made similar "promises"—and the resulting disappointment, heartbreak, and emotional damage left in the wake.

"A sad soul can kill you quicker, far quicker, than a germ."
-John Steinbeck

When I started this project/book, I had three major goals or purposes. The first was to honor such children as the girl and Timmy by sharing their stories. The last 35 plus years I have encountered many similar children with both horrendous and heroic stories and lives.

Hero is a word tossed around loosely these days, including people as diverse as sports and rock stars to soldiers and firemen. When I think of heroic behavior, Timmy and children like him come to mind as they have handled unbelievable abuse, seen countless horrors, overcome mammoth odds, and somehow survived due to their courage and resiliency. They, like the butterfly, have fought through the "pupa" stage, experienced the "chrysalis," and, although damaged, spread their wings and flew on with their lives.

I have heard their screams and seen their tears, but have always felt honored to have played a role, no matter how small, in their transitions and transformations. Very few people are as fortunate as I—as I get to work daily with such heroes.

The second purpose was to fill an unspoken commitment to the many people who have urged and encouraged me to initiate and complete this project. I include in this group grandparents, foster parents, adoptive parents, step parents, colleagues, parents, relatives providing care, siblings parenting siblings... all engaged in the critical and growing role of the "substitute parent." I have also received encouragement from the children themselves, clients and former clients who have expressed their hope that such a book might benefit the "substitute" parents and therefore have a positive impact on the children like them who are in care.

The third purpose or goal—the heart and soul of this book—was to provide tangible concrete assistance to those of you striving daily to help the "Timmy's" of the world get through the metamorphosis with minimum damage and as few screams as possible.

The most difficult challenge in the world is to be a "good parent." It is one of the few jobs or obligations we get into that does not come with an instruction manual. I would, however, argue that there does exist a more difficult challenge than the above... being a good "substitute" parent for someone else's child.

Those of you who have accepted this role are to be commended and deserve all of the help and support you can get.

Those of you considering this role need to be aware of the challenges you may face and the skills required to have a chance of being more productive and successful.

Those of you who were thrust or find yourself immersed in this substitute role may find more assistance in this book than the first two groups.

It is my fervent hope that you will find such assistance in the coming pages.

I have spent my entire adult life working with children, many like Timmy, who have been placed in out-of-home care, far too often meeting with little success. These children remind me of the nursery rhyme figure Humpty Dumpty, falling from the wall, hitting the pavement, busting into pieces, and sorely in need of the "King's men" to repair the damage. I have often asked myself, as well as colleagues, "How many more falls can this kid take until the damage is irreparable? How much courage does it take to get up and climb back up the wall again? Where are we going to find enough King's men who know how to repair the damage?"

Most of my professional career has been as a residential counselor for children ages six to eighteen years who have been placed outside of their homes due to neglect, abuse, sexual abuse, and other circumstances mostly outside of their control. The information provided within these pages has been accumulated and gleaned from numerous seminars, workshops, trainings, books, professional discussions, thousands of conversations with children, and, of course, good old fashioned experience.

The challenges are many, the problems seem to increase in number and complexity, while the resources shrink, and the screams of the butterflies continue to multiply.

Statistics vary depending upon the source of the information. When I first started compiling information in 2007, national figures indicated that at any given time there were over 500,000 children in foster care, over 200,000 being adopted each year, 1.7 million children in relative/kinship care, and approximately 40% of children under the age of 18 years were living with a "step parent." Costs of services for those in foster care and kinship care was estimated at over $10 billion.

In Indiana, my home state, in 2007 there were over 5,000 children in "substitute" care, most of who were in foster care placement with 4,300 licensed foster homes, as of 2007. Estimates are that in the course of a "normal" year Indiana has 11,000 children in care at a cost that exceeds $43 million.

Recent trends in Indiana and across the country have been to reduce the number of children in care, reduce the time in out-of-home placement, decrease residential placements and increase "kinship care" placements. Part of the impetus for these reductions is one of simple economics... the financial resources are not available as all government entities are caught in the financial bind of the times.

Statistics based on the AFCARS data (Adoption and Foster Care Reporting System) for 2010 indicate 408,000 children "in care" at the start, 53,000 adoptions, and 662,000 children served. Those are children in adoptive or foster care placements, this does not include relative or step parent care. Those numbers have dropped since 2002 with 523,000 "in care" 51,000 adopted, and 800,000 served. My educated guess for the decline is the emphasis on keeping children in their homes or seeking relative placement.

Statistics for relative and step parent care are even more difficult to get a good reading on based upon lack of information. Reporting requirements are nonexistent and, therefore, voluntary.

What is generally agreed on is that divorce rates are escalating (one out of every two marriages fail), which also produces more shared or substitute parents. In addition, we are now seeing that divorce rates amongst people in their second marriage are exceeding the rate of first marriage divorce (60%). The number one reason cited for divorce amongst these "blended" families is conflicts over parenting "step children."

The AFCARS data cited above indicates at least 30% of children are living in a step parent situation (I have seen data as low as 23% and as high as 50%) with three million children not living with either biological parent.

All of the above indicates there are a large number of children being parented by someone other than their biological parents. This parenting is often at the root of many divorces, and has serious consequences for the child and the family.

Some of you who provide such care actually asked for the role, some of you were trained to serve in this capacity, but most of you were thrust into this role, as was the child in care.

More and more grandparents, siblings, and other relatives are taking over for "moms and dads" unwilling, unable, and/or unavailable to parent, be it for a limited time or permanently. Being a grandfather of five delightful grandchildren (and we are eagerly awaiting number six who will join our family this year from the Congo) I have a particular empathy for you grandparents raising your second family, long after you thought your parenting trials and tribulations were over.

It is important to remember, although your role is difficult, very few of the children asked for this situation. They come into our homes and facilities with a multitude of concerns, needs, feelings, thoughts, and issues. They also come with expectations of you and hopeful they will get the best effort and care to assist in their adjustment to placement so they can get on in life.

Many of these children will be in your care for an unknown period of time. Foster care and residential placements are becoming briefer and briefer. Most will not be in your care permanently or even through their adolescence. These brief placements add to the difficulty for all involved and, therefore, require better skills and strategies by the "substitutes" involved. At times what I do—and you will find yourself doing—is "triage," like a M.A.S.H. unit in the armed forces. The immediate emergency care, the patching up, stopping the immediate pain/suffering, and then sending them on their way... at times back to where they were originally wounded.

It is my intention in the forthcoming pages to provide you with concrete information, skills, and strategies you can utilize for the benefit of the child in your care, "triage" as well as longer term care.

As previously stated, most of the information comes from my experiences, often learned the hard way by "trial and error," as well as by "trial and failure." My best teachers were the children with whom I worked and built relationships. To them I owe a huge debt.

Thank you for allowing me into your lives (when you were sick of meddling adults getting into your business). Thank you for being patient and kind when I made mistakes (traits seldom returned to you by many of the adults in your lives). Thank you for having the courage to set me straight when I was wrong (behavior you infrequently experienced being reciprocated by many). Thank you for showing the resiliency to climb back up on that wall and live life even though you had fallen before. Thank you for trying new ideas and skills, stepping out of old habits and comfort zones to improve your lives, and thank you for giving me a daily reminder of what it means to be HEROIC.

I was very fortunate to have had a few mentors already in the field when I was a "rookie" willing to lend a hand and especially an empathetic ear. I have also benefited from a number of dedicated professionals that I have met who shared invaluable lessons. You will recognize yourselves and your contributions throughout this book.

Reading has been a love of mine since I was a child and I have eagerly consumed literature in the field, jotting down notes, underlining passages, pulling out stories, quotes and ideas for future use. I have attended numerous seminars, workshops, and trainings that have provided tremendous help in doing my job. I have made a concerted effort to "pass along" some of the best I have encountered, hoping such will be relevant and useful in your role.

I especially want to acknowledge and thank the faculty and staff of the Family Life Development Center, College of Human Ecology, Cornell University's Residential Child Care Project for their pioneer work, training, and outstanding curriculum... Therapeutic Crisis Intervention (T.C.I.). I have been a certified "trained trainer" in

Cornell T.C.I. since 1988. Each training recertification has resulted in improved skills and ideas to utilize.

One of my former mentors, a veteran street-wise lady and tremendous case worker once advised me to watch closely and copy what she did. This lady had a great reputation with children, colleagues, foster parents, and the community in which she lived and worked. She wanted me to get ready to assume her role with these families and the children in her care. Being new and somewhat brash, I thought it best if I did things my way, a new and probably better way. However, I thought, "What the hell, I'll watch and see, she's been around a while and the kids like her." She was right. I observed, listened and asked questions... eventually doing as she suggested and copied many of her strategies and nuances. I did not adopt all as this lady carried a .25 caliber handgun in her purse and recommended I do the same!

The lesson most valuable gleaned from this experience was to be "eclectic." Listen, learn, and borrow generously from authors, trainers, experts, colleagues, and others... whoever makes sense and helps you improve. Be a "Robin Hood" of sorts, taking from those who know and give it to those who have yet to learn. Share the skills, share the experiences, failures as well as triumphs, and teach each child in your care all of the skills you possess so he or she can be more effective and better prepared for life. Encourage the child to be like "Robin Hood," observing others who do well and mimic those behaviors and strategies. Continuing to do the same thing over and over that has not worked makes no sense and will lead to exhaustion, if not resignation.

Those you hear complaining of "burn-out" have themselves to blame as they have failed to rekindle their own flame—stuck in a rut—rather than learning new skills and moving on down the road. To stave off "burn-out," fire up your learning skills and develop rather than stagnate. I believe it was Albert Einstein who said, "Insanity is doing the same thing over and over and expecting different results."

Taking a page from the Boy Scouts—Be Prepared. Taking this one step further—Be Prepared to Fail.

When I decided to make this course of study my life's work, my father asked me a simple question, "Gary, how are you going to deal with failure?" I had thought quite a bit about the work and success I felt I could have with children and their families. Quite frankly I had not given due consideration to the other side of the coin. He patiently explained that I was the type of person who liked being successful, to do well, to achieve, make a difference, and meet goals and objectives. He wondered out loud how I would handle failures, mine and those as well of my clients. Having taught and coached in public schools for over 30 years, as well as working with the children and families in the children's home, he had a pretty good idea about failure, children, families, and that success and progress were often not easily produced, immediately known, and incremental in nature.

My father's question that day gave me a lot to ponder and it has resonated over the years.

I pose the same question for your consideration.

The "failures" will be easy to note... success and progress are often not realized for years and usually in small increments. The "failures" tend to make the headlines and are the ones of which we see and hear. If you are deluding yourself about this role and your abilities as a "substitute" you will add to the "failures" and the burden will be carried by the children in your care more so than you.

The chapter titles come directly from the questions most often asked of me. Usually these questions come from people already enmeshed in the "substitute" parent role and they are distraught, worn out, grasping for help, and far too often guilt laden.

During the last 25 years I have averaged four to six inquiries a month from anonymous people seeking help and assistance as parents and "substitute' care givers. I also get the same questions from people I know who are teachers, parents, and relatives taking care of children.

Along with their specific questions the other two most popular ones posed to me are:

What is wrong with kids these days?

How do you manage to stay in this work? How can you handle the sorrow and turmoil?

I choose not to directly address either question as that is not the purpose of this book.

As to Question #1, everyone has an opinion on the subject and is usually happy to voice theirs. I, too, have an opinion and will briefly share mine in the conclusion.

This is not meant to be a political or philosophical treatise, nor is it a forum for my social commentary. I have geared these pages for the people struggling daily trying to do the best they can for the child in their care. My personal politics, philosophy, whatever, may serve to alienate someone who does not share such views. My aim is to have the reader focus on the content, the skills, the issues, and the strategies which have nothing to do with politics and are minimally influenced by social philosophy.

As to Question #2, I think my response will be obvious in the coming pages and I hope the stories of the children lead to your taking action on their behalf.

Suffice it to say, every day I work with children and their families and I am reminded of what it means to persevere and act with courage. I witness resiliency and bravery seldom displayed elsewhere. As a child I am not sure I could have withstood one tumble from the wall without shattering. I am pretty sure there is no way I possessed the courage to climb back up!

The stories are based on actual episodes and event with other children sharing their similar experiences. I would be pleased to use real names to honor those people, but have changed names, ages, sex, etc. out of respect for their privacy, and for professional ethics.

As to the sleeping girl, I did not know her name or what became of her. I maintained contact with Timmy and his sisters for some time but it has been over ten years since our paths have crossed. In the last contact we had with Timmy, he was doing well. He was working, supporting his family, and staying out of trouble with the law.

Every day I come to work and walk into the building I am reminded of the little girl, curled up on the bench, sleeping and perhaps dreaming of her parents. That memory and the image of a traumatized Timmy fiercely holding on to the front porch column, serve as reminders of my responsibilities to each and every child to prevent such occurrences in their lives, or at least decrease the screams and suffering of these butterflies.

In 1968 I remember Senator Robert F. Kennedy quoting the author, Albert Camus:

"Perhaps we cannot prevent this world from being one in which children are tortured and suffer. But we can reduce the number of tortured and suffering children. And if you the believers don't do this, who will."

I have kept a copy of that quote in every office I have worked to remind me of my obligations.

With this in mind, my fondest hope is that you too will be a believer. I want this book to help you do all you can, for whoever you can, as often as you can, for as long as you can, to the best of your abilities... to reduce the suffering, to reduce the torture, to improve the life of a child for the time you have been afforded, and perhaps to change the screams of the butterfly from pain and anguish to those of joy and laughter.

"Nobody makes a greater mistake than he who did nothing because he could only do a little."
- Edmund Burke

Best wishes in this pursuit...

Chapter 1:

"What kind of family will Sarah need? Are we that family?"

"The first bright step into the sunshine of life begins with the opening of the cocoon. The caterpillar becomes a butterfly spreading her wings into the world. What she is today is but a tiny mirror of the transformation that is yet to come. For with time, love, humor, and warmth she is an ever changing masterpiece."
-New Beginnings: A Flight In the Sun, *Linda Diet*

It was late, I was home, tired and ready to relax when the phone rang.

Phone calls after hours, late in the evening, when nothing personal is expected are usually not good news, and this one was no different.

On the other end was Mr. R, a prospective foster father who I had been in the process of licensing as a foster family. I had met earlier in the evening with him and his wife for dinner in their home and to discuss foster parenting and what their expectations were as well as ours, as an agency, and possibly the child coming into their home.

He informed me that he and his wife had just finished a long and rather bitter argument and he had come to the conclusion that he felt he could not offer what a child would need. Mrs. R, however, was insistent that not only could he do so he would do so in conjunction with her and all would work out once a child was in their home.

We talked about his concerns for fifteen minutes or so and agreed to meet, just the two of us, to discuss those concerns in private. When we met, he voiced some of the same feelings I had experienced immediately after the birth of our first child. He just was not sure he should get into this and was very concerned he would not measure up to being a "normal" Dad. He had doubts that he and his wife could provide the kind of family environment a child would need. Mr. R also felt it was only fair to voice such concerns prior to having a child placed, fail, then go through the pain of seeing the child removed.

Mr. R and I talked at length that day sitting in his car and later met with his wife the next week. In our open discussion we were able to get them to take a critical look at the new role they were about to undertake to help them determine if they were the people that could provide a substitute family for a child. They later did decide to do so, completed the licensing process, and for a number of years offered very good substitute care and eventually adopted two of the children placed when they became available.

I don't think Mr. R would have done so or could have done so without giving voice to his doubts and concerns and engaging his wife in a critical look at their family.

"Biology is least of what makes a mother." - Oprah Winfrey

Although there seems to be fewer and fewer consensus thoughts or feelings in our society, I think it is safe to say that most people would agree that families have undergone major radical changes over the last 30 to 40 years. What we used to consider a "normal family" hardly exists, and even those families that function fairly well would not label themselves as "normal." My guess is a family called "normal" could tell us any number of things that makes them feel anything but "normal"... if we could get them to stop laughing at the description. A coworker of mine for years has kept a notice posted outside his entry door that reads...

"We are all dysfunctional! Get over it!"

The family "models" of *Ozzie and Harriet, Leave it to Beaver* or even *Andy Griffith of Mayberry* (unconventional in his day) are almost extinct. The "blended" family such as the *Brady Bunch* is much more the norm, although the *Brady Bunch* would not be viewed as a typical "blended" family today.

Families look, feel, and function different in today's society. There are more of the "blended" variety as well as extended families. As noted in the introduction, the number of blended families is increasing as is the divorce rate of second marriages, 60% or higher. Two common reasons cited for these divorces are stepchildren issues and arguments. Want to guess what most of these arguments are about... the parenting of stepchildren.

Many of the blended families I have known do not paint a picture of a warm, harmonic collage. The stories I hear remind me more of a kitchen blender, with the top unsealed, where the carrots, tomatoes, juice, etc. are all suddenly thrown together, the power switch flipped on, and the chomping, spewing, cutting and grinding commence at full force. The result is seldom a tasty, attractive, healthy pureed tonic—more like an inedible and yucky mess.

More and more relatives, especially grandparents, are providing the basic family for children. There have been major increases in single parent and foster homes, to the point that the "non-traditional" family is, in fact, traditional.

We do know, regardless of the composition, children need a family to survive, grow, and prosper... it is the crucial element. Children need to have good role models who nurture, insure their safety, provide for their welfare, care, and comfort as well as offering a sense of self and belonging. Families that "do well" do well for reasons. Healthy families have certain characteristics that need to be considered, especially if it is your desire to provide care for other people's children.

Prior to making this commitment to be in the parental role it may benefit you to ask...

"Does our family do well enough to provide for Sarah?"

"Do we have the resources to open our family to Sarah?"

If the answer to the above is yes, the next question is: "How do we integrate Sarah into the family? What is it that families do that 'do well'?"

All families have problems and issues, and I am unaware of any guaranteed formula for success. However, there are characteristics that, when exhibited, indicate a decent level of functioning and offer a better chance for success with raising children.

As you review the following, do yourself and Sarah a favor, be honest in your self-appraisal. There is no sin in deciding your family is not the one for Sarah. It is far better for her and you to make that decision prior to accepting her into your home. Sarah and so many children have met with far too many rejections. A realistic look at your family may save her from one more "failed placement." I would caution those of you in second marriages to have the courage to pose this question: "If we bring

_____ into our home, what are the potential challenges we might face?" before proceeding to the other assessment questions.

We do know that Sarah has a better chance for success if placements are kept to a minimum. For relationships to be built it takes time, and moving from home to home offers little opportunity to build permanent relationships. A recent study conducted in the Midwest indicates two major reasons for foster children being successful. The first was the presence of one central adult who was continuously involved in the child's life; believe it or not this one person could be the child's case manager or social worker. The second essential factor to success was minimal numbers of placements. When a foster child has two or fewer placements while out of his own home, his chance of being successful greatly exceeds the child with three or more such placements. Those two factors were more important than intelligence, diagnosis, reason for placement, severity of behavior, educational status, or family background.

If Sarah can have one adult who is there for her consistently, who can be depended upon, if Sarah's placements can be limited to two or less, her chances of success are greatly enhanced.

I believe the correlation is obvious... Sarah with the above factors is in a situation that allows for building and sustaining relationships.

I hold true admiration for those of you offering care and support, opening your homes and lives to children like Sarah. You know best the reasons why you chose to do so, the pluses, the "warm fuzzies" so to speak, that doing this can bring into your life.

I do not wish to minimize such and I do not want to "scare" people away from providing this needed service.

Unfortunately, however, I have witnessed a large number of people and families, with the best of intentions, fail. Some have been adoptive families as well as step parent, relative, and foster families.

Most of those failures were due to a lack of planning, proactive thoughtful preparation, and unrealistic expectations placed on the child and themselves.

When these homes "disrupt," fail, or did not "work out," there is plenty of guilt and reasons for all to share. However, it is the child who shoulders most of the burden, blame, and pain. It is Sarah who suffers the most damage when her "new family" closes the door.

Such a loss can be very traumatic as most children see this as another case of being rejected and secretly ask, "What's wrong with me?"

Being prepared is vital. You need to take a realistic inventory of yourself and family prior to making this commitment. You can do more harm than good if you fail.

Early on in my professional career I was involved in the recruitment and licensing of new foster parents. I was also assigned a number of "step parent" adoptions which required home studies and interviews of the step parent with written recommendations for the Court.

During these encounters inevitably the new parent to be would comment as to his or her reasons for pursuing licensure or the adoption. Comments typically made would be, "I just love children," or "I have a lot to offer _____ ." I would at some point ask them if there were other ways they had considered to express their concern and respect for children rather than becoming adoptive or foster parents. I would caution all that parenting is difficult and not a position to be taken lightly. I was not surprised when I received a few astonished looks after those comments, but it was interesting to note how many people had not stopped to truly consider the ramifications on their or the child's life.

One of my supervisors took me to task for such comments as she felt I was being too negative in my portrayal of foster and adoptive parenting. I felt I was being realistic in the approach as many of the people had not thought about the "other side of the coin."

Parenting is not for everyone, and parenting someone else's child can be an extremely more daunting challenge.

Taking on a parental role and failing can lead to more than one person falling on their rear... failure may indeed bruise our adult egos, but absolutely devastate a child.

I realize many of you in the substitute parental role have situations that develop that do not always allow the luxury of preparation and proactive planning time.

Others, who are more fortunate, do have time to prepare and plan ahead.

Regardless, the following checklist will assist you in getting yourself ready and setting the situation up for success.

For a lack of a better term I will call it …

"OUR FAMILY" CHECKLIST:

1) Is your relationship with your spouse/partner strong and secure? Are you both committed to providing parental care?

Unfortunately I have witnessed too many marriages fall apart due to a lack of commitment by one of the parties involved. Some marriages have made the mistake of bringing a child into the family to "shore up" the relationship. If you are not secure and committed to one another, there is no way you can be secure and committed to a child to the degree necessary. Children will put a strain on the best of relationships, including biological children. Married couples raising a child have to rely upon each other in ways they never have in the past. Time and energy, resources we need in our relationship, get used and exhausted by any child. Be sure this is what you both want and you are committing to this endeavor together, otherwise all will suffer. Take time to discuss ways and means to keep your relationship as a major priority, as it is very easy to "live for the child," at the expense of each other.

2) Is your family, both immediate and extended, committed to this endeavor? What kind of support system do you have in place, i.e. friends, neighbors, church, etc. What can be expected from all of the above parties?

It is essential that everyone living in your family have a say as to accepting another person in the household as all will have a part to play and sacrifices to make. This simply means all need to be consulted openly, with their thoughts and feelings being given due consideration. This includes other children in the home. They will bring a different perspective to the discussion and endeavor, and may provide insight as to what the new child will feel and need. I strongly recommend, especially in foster and adoptive homes, that your youngest child be older than the child you are introducing to your family. You will want your child or children to be the model, rather than Sarah being their model. Having a younger new child also provides you with the experience in what to expect, as you have already parented at least one child through this developmental stage.

Often children like Sarah have seen and experienced things beyond your child's knowledge or age range (simply being in out of home care is traumatic). Those behaviors exhibited by foster and adoptive children may include anger, sexual acting out, aggression, and profanity, just to name a few. The safety of your child also comes into play with the age, size, and developmental stage of Sarah needing your consideration.

If your youngest child is older than Sarah he can assist you in the introduction of your home and family to Sarah. An older child can also be a better advocate for himself as well as Sarah, and in most cases can serve as a role model. Your child, if older, also has a better chance of understanding and tolerating Sarah, at least more so than if the roles were reversed.

One family I worked with in the preparation stage of foster care thought they were ready to open their home to a fourteen year old young man, who they had known through school contacts. The family's children liked the young man and were in favor of placement. During one of our discussions their twelve year old son admitted that he did have a concern. He expressed some worry about sharing his video games with the new boy. As this was discussed, it became obvious to all that the young man's concern had more to do with sharing his dad's time (he and dad routinely challenged each other in video games) than actually sharing his games and controllers. This led to further discussion on important matters such as how do we share our parents' time, as the introduction of another teen meant less individual time with the parents. Talking about the video game was a "safe" way of bringing up a concern their son had. Many adults would have either admonished their son for being "selfish" or immediately set about drawing up a schedule for video game time... neither of which were the core concern being expressed.

As the parent, it is your responsibility to get the opinions and feelings of all immediate family members as they will be most affected. It might take a little prodding for them to reveal some of their feelings and thoughts, in particular the children.

Be sure to involve your extended family and friends as their acceptance of Sarah is critical and their support could be a valuable resource. Extended family members that you have routine contact with need to be consulted and express their willingness to play their part. You may encounter a family member not thrilled with the idea, or unwilling to be supportive. This makes life more difficult for you and Sarah. You will need to explore if this person can, at least, agree to be cordial and not play a negative role? You may find some members not negative but reluctant and concerned. If so, take the time to talk this out prior to bringing Sarah into your family. Again, it has been my experience that a negative relative can make life miserable for Sarah and you. A reluctant relative with concerns may be "won over" with time and patience, especially if this person can be cordial and friendly to Sarah in her presence.

Pay attention to the feedback you receive from family and friends. Don't blow it off with the idea you and your immediate family can handle it all on your own.

Families that I have seen have the most success are those families that do the foundation work of preparation with immediate family members as well as extended members and friends.

3) Is your family a "supportive group?" Do you support each other in times of need, stress, and crisis? Do you support each other in pursuit of personal and professional goals and interests? Do you tend to look out for each other? Do you take interest in each other's activities?

As Sarah enters your family, one of the first things she will note is how you treat each other and if that support will be extended to her.

4) How does your family communicate? Does everyone get a chance to voice his or her opinion? Do members pay attention and truly listen to each other? Is there an atmosphere of encouragement to do one's best? Is your family environment a POSITIVE or NEGATIVE environment?

Previous studies have indicated that families that do well exude a positive environment. One study reported that a positive family environment is one in which for every negative comment there are 20 positive comments, a 20 to 1 ratio. No doubt that is an exceptional ratio, but it points out the importance of positive expression over negative remarks and how such helps build healthy families.

Positive families are based on a democratic model, not autocratic. Honest communication is the norm. Everyone gets a chance to be heard. Decisions are made after considering all points of view, and are subject to reconsideration. The rights of all are protected, youngest as well as oldest.

5). Does your family spend time together, share tasks, plan fun outings, EAT together and enjoy each other's company?

These are all characteristics of a healthy family. Believe it or not, eating together is very important and family therapists highly recommend a minimum of four to five meals together weekly.

In conversations I have had with children and parents I have always been amazed at how little importance they give to dining together as a family. The interesting thing I have learned from many meals shared at our facility is how much children like to have adults interact at meal time. When we plan a cookout or special dinner we have more residents volunteer to help than at any other time. At any meal if a member of the staff who does not have to be present in the dining room walks in, requests go up from numerous tables for that person to sit down and share a meal.

I realize children and adults have busy schedules, we did, too, when our children were in school; high school in particular. We almost always cooked more than we knew we needed as our children understood it was fine to bring other kids home to eat, as long as they made the meal time. We had quite a few late dinners, and the local pizza place at one time recognized my wife's voice without giving her name, as we called in quite often once the total party was counted for dinner. There were very few problems with this arrangement, and we really got to know with whom our children were associating. We became very fond of many of their friends and to a lesser degree grieved their loss when our kids went on to college.

The important aspect here is spending time together as a family, be it a meal, movie, activity, or church… whatever it is, do it together. I will be surprised if your new child is not surprised at the quality and quantity of time your family spends enjoying yourselves.

6) Does your family have a ways and means of resolving difficulties, a problem solving mechanism or method that provides safety and full participation?

When the going gets tough and tense, how does your family respond? Do you compromise and collaborate, or does one member take control, make the decision and dictate the plans?

In the case of many of the children we see in out of home care, they have come from families who also have a ways and means of resolving conflicts. Unfortunately, these methods are often unhealthy, unsafe, and irrational (except in their minds) and meet the needs of the primary adult in the home without consideration for the child. In fact, families that break up or implode can quite often trace the reason for such to their problem solving methodology.

7) Does your family respect the rights of the individual? What are the privacy issues or boundaries in your family? Is each member treated with dignity and respect?

Many children coming into substitute parental care have lived in situations where privacy was undervalued and the rights of the individual were not as important as the need of the adults. In the extreme case this can be seen in sexual abuse and incest of children by parents, relatives, boyfriends, and unfortunately with less than desirable caregivers whom the parents have left the children in care.

Boundaries are very important for children as is the right to privacy. Boundaries provide safety, security, and limits while privacy provides respect, time, and space.

Establishing and defining boundaries for Sarah may be a totally new experience for her and will need extra work on your part.

8) Is your family flexible? Is it capable (especially the adult members) of adapting and handling transitions with minimal stress and conflict?

Any addition to an established family will cause change and flux simply by adding one more body to the space available. All will need to adapt and flex as various issues are worked through and accommodations are made. The parents must be the leaders and models of adaptation and flexibility.

Accommodations such as Sarah's family involvement, visitations, therapists appointments, caseworkers, mentors, new friends, schedules being adjusted, space and time sharing, school changes, are just a few of the transitions that will be faced almost immediately within your family.

"Be flexible—dinosaurs became extinct because they did not adapt."
-Anonymous

One issue of flexibility and adjustment that comes with foster, relative, and group home caretakers is the ordeal of saying goodbye. When we are engaged in parenting someone else's child it is usually a temporary situation. Face it, Sarah is going home sooner or later, and we need to be cognizant and start planning for that moment when she first crosses our threshold. In most cases, Sarah will leave sooner than we feel she is ready and return to the family from where she came. We have accepted the challenge to totally invest in her life for the short time we have her, and then say goodbye and good luck.

I have witnessed a number of great foster parents and child care workers simply wear out due primarily to this fact of life. I use the term "wear out" as the constant coming and going can wear you down physically and emotionally.

My objective with every child I have worked with is to build a relationship, increase his skills, functioning, self-esteem, school effort, and anger management, whatever... to the OPTIMAL level of performance during his tenure. This OPTIMAL level may very well be below standards I would like to see him achieve, but with this approach, the interventions and efforts, I can assist him in being better prepared to carry on in life. It has also helped me to remind myself there will be another child coming through the door as the last one leaves who deserves my best efforts.

I make it a point to remind the child departing that I am available to help if the need would arise. I leave the burden on him to contact me, hopefully leaving the door open for further contact. I actually hear from quite a few after they have left our agency.

In this line of work, when you open your home and your heart to a child, "parting," to paraphrase Shakespeare, can "be such sweet sorrow."

9) Is your family tolerant? Tolerant of others and each other? Do you accept the differences amongst each member? Do you look for common ground and celebrate diversity? Are you forgiving of each other's errors and human foibles?

Tolerance is another attribute that children coming into our care may lack. Often they have seen little tolerance practiced by the adults in their family and life, either towards others or with them. Intolerance can be a family tradition.

A young man named Lenny, age 14, came from such a tradition. He had major difficulties getting along with people of a different race. During one of our counseling sessions I challenged him to change his thinking in regard to race. He looked at me like I was one of the stupidest people he had met, or at least encountered as a counselor. Lenny quickly set me straight, "Gary, you don't get it! My grandpa hated _____, my dad hates _____, and I do, too!" Regardless of this rebuff I continued to work with Lenny on his thinking, not tackling the racial views expressed, but taking on other areas where he was a little more likely to try a different approach. My hope was if I could get him to change some distorted thinking he might eventually come around to reconsidering his thinking on racial matters. I wanted Lenny to at least accept responsibility for his feelings, thoughts, and behavior rather than laying them at the feet of his ancestors. Once he took responsibility for some feelings, thoughts, and the behavior his thoughts fueled, he might choose to change those ingrained beliefs.

Tolerance has to be taught and modeled. With Lenny I had to "tolerate" (put aside my feelings) of his intolerance to begin to build a working relationship that hopefully would include addressing his bias.

During a training exercise over twenty years ago I had a child care worker interrupt my presentation to exclaim, "You know, Gary, what you are saying is this... it is like our kids have little video cameras taped to their heads. What they see, they film, then play it back to us fifteen minutes later." This comment was right on target.

> *"Be the change you want to see.*   *-Gandhi."*

10) Does your family have a sense of humor? Can you laugh at yourself as well as with each other? Is everything "serious business," or can you look at the lighter side?

As with many of the above characteristics, children coming into placement have not experienced a lot of joy, fun, or humor in their short lives. The humor they have seen displayed has been at the expense of others, including their being the butt of the joke or target for ridicule. Joy is a foreign concept or, at best, a rarely experienced phenomenon. I have had many adults tell me that "Sarah does not seem to enjoy anything," with the observation appearing to be valid. Sarah and others have had to grow old without being allowed to be a child. You may be the one adult who introduces her to fun and humor.

It is important to show Sarah that you are human, so when you goof up, admit it. Laugh at yourself. Recently at breakfast I spilled gravy down the front of my shirt. The three boys sitting at the table noticed immediately but did not say anything. I quickly commented, "Geez, with a mouth as big as mine how can I miss it with a fork?" We all had a good laugh and they shared similar stories and embarrassing moments.

I was advised years ago by a very dear older lady who had spent years working with and for children not to take myself too seriously. Her words were, "Sometimes you just have to laugh to simply keep from crying." No doubt you will find plenty to bemoan and cry about in this field, enjoy the moments when laughter can erupt.

I realize I have listed ten characteristics important in families wanting to provide "substitute" care, but have not included material resources, i.e. money, house, etc.

Those fail to make my top ten list as I have not found the lack of those things truly preventing people who wanted to provide care from doing so. Some of the best money managers I knew were the least wealthy foster parents.

It is expected that there will be real costs anytime you increase your family size, but the resources needed the most are **Time** and **Patience**.

People, especially busy people, like to talk about "quality time" as opposed to "quantity time." It seems parents are more concerned about getting the most out of the little time they have parenting, i.e. quality time. However, time, like anything else, depends upon your perspective.

How long a minute is depends on which side of the bathroom door you are on.

Children do not think in terms of quality of time, or money. They think more in terms of how much time you spend with them, and what that time is used for. Do they get their fair share of attention during the time frame seems more important than the actual time.

Quality demands quantity... when involved with children.

"Children need our presence more than our presents." -Jesse Jackson

A luxury sedan you may purchase is a quality automobile, but only because of the time and effort it took to manufacture the sedan. Design time, test time, manufacture time, quality assurance time, etc. all large amounts of time go into such automobiles, increasing the value.

Masterpieces of any sort require quantity of time as well as quality of effort. Michelangelo painted masterpieces only because he took the time and was careful with every stroke of the paint brush.

Children like Sarah (in my opinion any child) are going to require more of your resource of time.

The other resource is Patience. Patience, of course, involves time, usually quantity more so than quality.

As in the case of Michelangelo I doubt every brush stroke went on as he designed or desired. From all accounts, he, like many other talented people, spent numerous hours scraping, patching, reworking, and repainting before he unveiled the ceiling of the Sistine Chapel.

The same is true for Sarah. What your biological child might have picked up in two easy lessons or steps might take constant repetition before she can add it to her skill repertoire. Reassurance is a key element in working with other people's children. Remember you are not only trying to implant new skills, you are in the process of helping Sarah discard old reliable skills that may have been unhealthy and irrational.

Sarah will have to test her new skills and if found lacking to meet her needs, it is very likely she will fall back on her old ways of doing things... leaving you to start over in the teaching and encouraging modes. If a new skill does indeed work, Sarah may use it some of the time and disregard it at other times. This can be very frustrating for you in your role and you will need to persevere.

Those of you who have taught or coached can relate to the above.

I met with similar frustrations when teaching my children to drive. One of the necessary steps is to use your right foot only for braking and acceleration. However with a new driver, the urge is to use the left on the brake and the right on the accelerator. On country roads with no traffic, things went smoothly. However, once we entered a more congested driving area, both of my children had a tendency to let the left foot creep onto the brake. I am sure this gave them a more secure feeling, one of better control over the car. However, in reality it was not a safe way to drive a car regardless of the traffic. It took time and patience of the teacher, in this case me, before either would routinely adjust and utilize the new skill. After doing so, with plenty of reminders from me to keep their left foot off of the brake, both adjusted and drove without further problems. The new skill was not mastered in one lesson, it took time and patience. I am sure my children have different recollections of the learning process and may not have the same perception as to my degree of patience, but the example is germane.

When you are engaged with Sarah and learning a new skill, remember... skills take time, practice, and patience. Reflect on your experience in learning something new. What worked best for you? Who were your great teachers? How did they teach?

My guess is your experiences were similar to most of us; our great teachers were probably similar in three critical areas;

1) They spent the time necessary to teach us and built a "teaching" relationship.

2) They were patient with us when we failed to learn.

3) They "broke down" the learning experience into incremental steps we could climb and set up some form or fashion of reward if only a brief "good job."

Sarah will require all three of the above in your efforts. Those are invaluable resources we can all give, if willing.

A study conducted in Australia from 1999 to 2007, supports the above statements. This study conducted by the Family Strengths Research Project looked at characteristics or behavior traits of "happy" families, regardless of their economic situation or social status. The study indicated there were eight traits common to families who do well.

1) Communication is a two way process based on understanding and patience.

2) Shared activities.

3) Togetherness.

4) Support, members are there for each other and take time for the family as a whole as well as for individual members.

5) Affection.

6) Acceptance, the sense of being wanted and belonging.

7) Commitment, both of time and trust.

8) Resilience, the ability to handle stress, problems, and overcome obstacles.

It is going to be very important with Sarah that you focus, at least initially, on Communication, Support, Acceptance, and Commitment.

Communication and support are addressed throughout this book but a few words need mentioning on acceptance and commitment.

Acceptance indicates a willingness on your part to have her join your family as she is, without immediate demands or expectations of major changes.

Will you accept Sarah as she looks, talks, dresses, wears her hair, i.e. the superficial issues? Will you accept Sarah's family and friends, often a more difficult commitment than dealing with the superficial issues?

The chances of her reaching her potential in your care are slim if you do not accept her at the start where she is and treat her the way you want her to become. Respect her feelings, opinions, roots, culture, beliefs, and intelligence. Respect does not mean agreement. You can respectfully disagree with many people's opinions but still respect them as a person.

Avoid hypocrisy. Believe me, Sarah and children in her position are on the lookout for you to do something you have told them not to do. Practice what you preach, preach as little as possible, and let your behavior indicate your beliefs and values.

Don't do harm. Remember Sarah or any child is just that, a child. Recognize that Sarah and many of the children we see have experienced trauma. She is not a product, project, problem, or a diagnosis. Treat her like you would want to be treated.

It is my hope that the preceding pages have assisted you and your family in an assessment of characteristics, strengths, motivations, and overall functioning of your family. Maybe this assessment has been surprising in that you have discovered assets in your family that had not been recognized or acknowledged. Maybe the reverse has been the case, but if so, you now have a better idea as to what needs rethinking, reworking, more consideration, and or improvement.

My goal was not to "talk you out" of providing care. In fact, I hope you have decided to pursue the role of substitute parent and now have a better grasp of what it takes to be a "family" to Sarah and other children in similar circumstances.

"Call it a clan, call it a network, call it a tribe, call it a family. Whatever you call it, whoever you are, you need one."
-Jane Howard

Chapter 2
What do I say after I say "Hello?" What is Johnny thinking?

"The great purple butterfly
 In the prison of my hands
Has a learning in his eye
 Not a poor fool understands."
-William Butler Yeats

Seth, although fifteen years old and having spent a good deal of his youth on the streets and in and out of shelters with his mother, was scared, or at the very least anxious, when he walked into our facility his first day. Like almost all of our residents, he had not been consulted about his placement and did not want to be here.

He said very little and responded mostly with grunts and one word responses, all the while hunkering over and keeping his "hoodie" pulled up to his mouth. I could barely make out his features due to the length of his hair, which was very long on the sides and hanging over most of his face. I could see his eyes, although cast down, as well as his nose, but that was pretty much it.

Seth continued to "hunker down," avoided eye contact, kept to himself, and was always wearing his "hoodie" up to his mouth and clenched in his teeth. I knew he had some severe developmental issues and that it would take time and perseverance to make inroads into his life.

Finally after about a week he agreed to let me take him to his home so he could secure some of his few belongings. He and his mother, never anyone else, were living in a small two room apartment off an alley. Seth, still a man of few words, did let me know he did not want me going into the apartment, although his mother was quite vocal in wanting my help moving his things. I abided by his wishes, only taking things from the door to the van as things were handed to me.

On the way home I asked Seth why I could not come in and he told me, "I didn't want you to see how dirty it was, you would think bad of my mom." I tried briefly to assure him that I did not judge someone by the cleanliness of their apartment as I did not want people to judge me by my looks or my home on certain hectic days.

This led to a limited discussion about looks, perceptions, etc., which in turn led to discussing his hair, "hoodie" and always hiding his face, especially his mouth.

Seth was able to confide that his hair hid his face and he kept his "hoodie" up to his mouth due to the poor condition of his teeth. They were protruding and snarled, to say the least, and had not been cleaned or treated, probably for years. His hair, clothes, and hoodie kept the focus away from his face as he did not want anyone to see him. He had been subjected to ridicule by his peers. He was embarrassed for himself and the reflection on his mother.

It took about a week but I finally convinced Seth to go and see a hair stylist. He did not have to commit to getting it cut or trimmed, this was an informal talk with the stylist. I had called a stylist I knew who worked at a local shop that we used regularly. She had agreed to "chat" Seth up and show him a few styles that might get the process started. Angie, the stylist, was very good at her craft and an excellent "chatter upper". She soon had him in the chair getting a wash and rinse. With his hair wet and pulled back it was the first time I had really seen his face as a whole.

Of course Angie's remarks carried a whole lot more weight than mine, and she was able to convince him he had great features being hidden by his hair, especially pronounced cheek bones. She also discussed how a trim could really accent those positive features and people would notice his "good looks". Long story short, one trim led to a more radical cut which led to his agreeing to go with me to see an orthodontist to begin restructuring of his teeth. Within one week of the first trim, Seth was actually smiling and soon abandoned his "hoodie in mouth, hunkered over" look.

Seth made more progress after he left our program and went into foster care. Clothing, hair style, etc. all became more mainstream for a fifteen year old, and I did not recognize him at school later in the year, he had to speak to me first. The transformation was something to behold, not just in his outward appearance but the impact on his self-esteem and overall functioning. The butterfly was slowly coming out of his cocoon and looking for his place in the sun.

Children such as Seth coming into your home are going to have similar issues, and their appearances may not be to your taste or standards.

Such superficial issues should not be forgotten, but also not your first priority when a youngster is first introduced to your home. Kids like Seth expect criticism from adults and do not expect to be accepted. In fact, most look for rejection, as that is familiar territory.

These children like Seth have a lot on their minds and many questions bouncing around in their heads. Those questions often involve safety, family, privacy, school, friends, rules, length of placement, and personal care.

Some of the first questions posed by children over the years are varied and depend upon what they know about you, the reason they were placed, age, sex, developmental age, intelligence, where they were before they came to you, etc. Typical questions posed are:

Where am I?

Who are you?

Why did this happen to me?

How long will I be here?

Does my family know I am here?

When will I see my family?

When can I go home?

When can I call home?

Am I in trouble?

Who else lives here?

Where will I go to school?

Can I see my friends, (boy and girl friends are always on the mind of adolescents)? Where do I sleep?

Where is the bathroom?

Will I have my own bed/bedroom?

Who is in charge?

Who is the boss?

If I don't like it do I have to stay?

What are the rules?

What do you want from me?

Are there other kids here?

When do we eat?

Underlying these questions are the big concerns Johnny has as to his being safe, provided for, concern about his family, and what is going to happen to him in the future.

If you have not met Johnny prior to his coming into your home, prepare yourself as the package he comes wrapped in might not be the package you particularly care for. His appearance may surprise or upset you. Do not over react. What he wears, the color of his hair, tattoos, piercing, etc. need to be viewed by you as superficial issues... it is just his surface and may give you a message he does not intend.

As was the case with Seth, your immediate reaction and introduction will determine for the most part, Johnny's perceptions of you, your home, and your family within the first few minutes of your encounter.

To Johnny, as was true with Seth, his appearance, clothes, hair, etc. may be the only things he brings with him from home and may be of paramount importance. There may also be reasons for all that don't necessarily meet your eye.

Remember, he is facing almost a total change in his life. Leave the superficial issues alone if at all possible, try to be as accepting as you can, and make adjustments as you go. If there is a major obvious problem, such as Johnny wearing a shirt that proudly proclaims, "Shit happens," address it as immediately as you can, maybe before he showers and turns in his dirty laundry, as to where and when he can wear this shirt.

The same holds true for music, reading material, etc. Your influence can be exerted with time, however, if Johnny is faced with dictatorial demands to change appearance, you are choosing to throw down the gauntlet and engage to enrage…

As he gets more comfortable in your home and with you he will be more amenable to changing some of the superficial issues. At times all it takes is the offer... "Hey, are you wanting a haircut, new shoes, clothes, etc." Most changes Johnny makes will be incremental in nature.

"If you smile at me I will understand,
Cause that is something everybody, everywhere
does in the same language."
-Wooden Ships, Crosby, Stills, and Nash

Start your initial encounter with a smile and an open inviting stance, followed with a sincere, "Hello, Johnny, welcome to our home." Next introduce yourself and those present with an invitation such as, "I'm _____, come on in and let's get acquainted. We can talk a few minutes, I'll show you around, and try to answer any questions you may have."

I do not recommend any physical contact beyond a handshake. Do not be surprised or offended if Johnny chooses not to shake your hand. If so, ignore this response and proceed. If he chooses not to sit, remain standing and start your conversation on the same eye level.

Ask Johnny if you have his name right and is that what he wants to be called. Let him know he can call you by... whatever you want to be called, Mom, first name, Mr. or Mrs. My recommendation is to tell him he can refer to everyone in the home by first name, or if he so desires, now or in the future, he can call you "mom, dad." Without being intrusive, it helps to ask him if he is experiencing any pain or discomfort. Again keep your inquiry non-invasive. This sets the tone for your concern and future dealings with Johnny.

This also opens up the discussion to possible health or medical conditions of which you need to be aware. I usually start this line of questioning with, "Hey, are you thirsty, need to use the bathroom?" then go on to allergies; food likes and dislikes, asthma, eyeglasses, etc. If you are aware of a condition or issue, don't ask, simply acknowledge the concern in private, that you understand Johnny at times has trouble getting to the bathroom at night and occasionally wets the bed. Let him know how you and he, together if needed, will handle such occasions.

He needs reassurance that he and his concern will be treated with respect and dignity.

Eliminate distractions, television, pets, phones, other children, when setting up the first meeting so Johnny feels he is receiving your complete attention. A caseworker or social worker making the placement can wait a few minutes to talk with you. Johnny is priority #1.

When you talk with the caseworker, or whoever brought Johnny to your home, do so if at all possible with him present. This establishes trust, confidence, and an atmosphere of integrity... where a person does not talk behind another person's back. If the caseworker wants to bring up difficult subjects that would cause Johnny discomfort or worry, ask them to call you later, you are more concerned about his feeling welcome and at ease.

Recognize that he may be confused or perplexed and you do not expect him to remember everything being talked about at the time of placement.

Be sure Johnny knows he can ask any question on his mind at any time during your talk. Remind him there is no such thing as a stupid question. You might not have an immediate answer, but reassure him you will look into the matter the first chance you get.

Remember... no matter how old, how tough, or how sophisticated Johnny might appear, what he is experiencing is traumatic. At the very least it is a major transition to an unknown situation, and we all fear the unknown.

I recommend getting him up and moving with a tour of the house and yard as soon as possible. This affords him an opportunity to see things as they are, rather than how he has been told or may be envisioning. Walking and talking helps the conversation flow, and can stimulate questions. It also provides Johnny with a visualization of the home or a "map" so to speak... where he will sleep, eat, the bathroom, your room. etc.

As you move through the house you can again ask the questions as to using the bathroom and privacy issues. He can drop his clothes and belongings off in his room and get a look at "his space" while you emphasize his right to his own area. Going through the kitchen offers an opportunity to discuss meals, snacks, drinks, and can help you get some ideas on his likes and dislikes.

This orientation tour is also an introduction to family rules or ways and means. It is important to keep it simple, and the younger the child, the simpler things need to be. Bear in mind that most people lose their ability to follow a conversation and have difficulty remembering what is to be done after points 1,2,and 3, or A, B, C. Assure Johnny that you will talk again tomorrow or later and go over a lot of the same things. He does not have to remember all that was mentioned.

It may help you to keep two acronyms in mind when talking with Johnny, or for that matter most any child you do not know...

K.I.S.S. – Keep your rules few and keep them simple

Keep

It

Simple

Stupid

The rules in your household should reflect your VALUES and set standards for the HEALTH, SAFETY, and WELL BEING of all members. The fewer the rules, the better. The more simply they are framed, the easier to remember and follow. If you can frame those rules in one sentence or a few brief words... good for you.

If you can frame your "rules" in terms of boundaries and parameters, you will be in better shape. Most young people I know see rules as things to break, whereas boundaries are lines of demarcation, and parameters provide choice and movement within a framework.

The language you use in stating your rules/parameters needs to be POSITIVE in nature; emphasize the 'do' rather than the 'don'ts'. "Johnny, in our home there is no need to lock the bedroom doors," rather than "Johnny, don't lock your bedroom door." 'Do' statements allow for an exchange; 'Don't" statements appear non-negotiable.

I make an attempt to meet with every new resident as soon after admission as possible to discuss what I have termed...

ELEPHANTS AND RABBITS

The elephants are the BIG rules, the ones that if violated people could get in serious trouble, get hurt, and possibly jeopardize placement. I have four such elephants that involve violence, school attendance, talking with adults, and respect for other people, their space and property.

The younger the child (don't forget developmental age is more important than chronological age), the more concrete we must be in our verbal instructions. Rules need to be limited to a few major principles, simple, and easy to recall. When I first meet a new resident and inform them that we have lots of rules, a few important rules I call elephants, and the many other I call rabbits. This comment usually gets his attention, "Elephants? Rabbits?"

I explain if you are stepped on by an elephant, it is serious injury. If you trip over a rabbit, you can usually bounce back up pretty quickly and go on with little damage.

Our "elephants" are:

1) No violence

2) Go to school each day

3) Talk with an adult if you are upset or need something

4) Respect other people's space, body, and belongings.

The rabbits, although important, are rules that if violated have consequences but are not likely to result in injury, harm, or in our case, discharge from placement.

Most children and very few of us adults can remember every rule, violation, and restriction in a placement facility. It is hard to identify and remember the names of 100 rabbits, whereas four elephants are a little more manageable.

Don't assume anything. Assuming makes an ASS of u and ME!!

It is easy, especially those of us with years of experiences, to take certain things for granted. If you have worked with 200 fifteen year old boys, #201 is going to be similar…WRONG! Each child is unique in his own way. Making assumptions can lead to mistakes, some of which can be rectified, others cannot.

A few years back we had a new young man come in to our facility. He was fifteen years old and had just been with us a few days when he requested to be a server in the dining room. Andre wanted to help and I assumed he knew how, so without thinking I said, "Sure, you can serve tonight." When I walked by the dining room I noticed that Andre had set one spoon and one bowl at each place… no other utensils were on the tables. Knowing we were having a big meal, not a snack, I realized this would not suffice. When I asked Andre why he had just put one spoon and one bowl per place, he responded, "That's all we use at my house." I assumed he knew how we set the table; he assumed his way of doing it was fine. I helped Andre finish setting the table and worked with him through the meal to avoid other problems and supported his effort. He became a very good reliable server who enjoyed helping out.

Not everything you are told about a child will turn out to be accurate. It is wise not to rely too much on what you are told and risk making false assumptions based on faulty information.

We had two teenage girls placed one day after lunch. It was obvious from their behavior and reports we received that both were less than intellectually gifted. The term "borderline" was used. It did not take us too long to discover that "borderline" was being generous. These girls had been in foster care for over a year so we as a staff ASSUMED they knew certain things and could function in a family setting. At dinner time we learned another lesson on assuming. At that, time we dined in a family style manner at large round tables, Karen and Sharon sat at the table where I was sitting for dinner. When we passed the gravy to Karen she stuck her face in the bowl and started "lapping the gravy," much like a dog at its water dish.

Meanwhile Sharon took the mashed potatoes, scooped out her helping with her hands and started eating with her fingers. We, staff and residents, were stunned. These girls had been in foster care for over twelve months… we assumed they knew how to eat at a family table.

They were surprised that we were surprised, but with time, patience, and much practice they learned new skills, one of which was how to use eating utensils. Having learned this lesson at dinner we avoided other hard lessons and embarrassments for the girls. We started all skills at the beginners level, from washing their hands, combing hair, on up through deodorant and feminine hygiene issues (of which they had no clue). After months of work they were able to go on to more appropriate foster homes and did well.

As you do the "walking and talking tour", you are engaging the child as well as providing information and beginning to add structure as he is getting a sense of what is important in your family and how "stuff" gets done—the parameters in your home. This can be a great opportunity to key in on important matters such as privacy, personal space, integrity, schedules, sharing meals, and how Johnny blends in to it all.

This orientation will work better and have more impact if done together as a team with your partner... if at all possible. You can do parts by yourself that seem more appropriate to your role, i.e. "dad" might want to take on personal hygiene with Johnny, but be sure to meet with Johnny together when discussing major rules and values. This conveys to him that you both feel adamant on upholding these major values.

This is especially crucial in the step-parent role!! As a step-parent or a relative acting in the parental role it is very important to get everyone on board. That would include the "real parents" if in the picture, the "other parent" not in the step-parent relationship, and family members who are actively involved. The more adults available for the child to protest to or attempt to "split", the more complicated this can get. Understand that even the best of children are masters at the technique of splitting!!

Splitting is a child's way of deploying the strategy of divide and conquer. The child will find out how parents feel on a particular issue and utilize this knowledge to manipulate either or both to get what it is he wants. This happens in almost everyone's family at one time or the other, but it can be extremely disruptive and deteriorate relationships in foster, step, and relative families.

When you want to make important points like these, be sure you are congruent in your delivery. Make eye contact, speak directly and clearly, and ask for understanding. For example, if I am explaining to Johnny a major family value or rule, I want to stop walking, turn to him, get eye contact, and say, "Johnny, before we enter one another's bedrooms or the bathroom, we knock and wait for a response. Privacy is important to all of us, and we need to respect each other's space. Do you have any questions about this? Good, so when I need to come into your room expect me to knock and get your permission, OK?"

Using the example of his space and privacy being honored by you will reinforce how important this is to all, and that he counts, too.

Again I would not overload him during the introduction but you can emphasize the few major rules of the home and family.

Answer all questions posed by him to the best of your ability. If you don't know, say so. Let Johnny know that you will keep him up to date on all matters that pertain to him and affect the family. I say something like this, "I will let you know what I know when I know it, and tell you the truth as I know it to be. Realize, I can be wrong at times, I make mistakes, but I will not lie or conceal the truth."

Be cautious and considerate with your personal questions. This is not the time, nor have you developed the relationship, to ask probing personal questions. If Johnny steers the conversation into family or personal areas, let him talk, listen attentively, and acknowledge the feelings behind the disclosure.

Easier questions can be asked that are geared at his comfort and getting him through the initial few days. Questions such as… do you sleep with a light on, or radio playing, (if so get him either for his use). What kind of foods and drinks do you like? What is your favorite television show, sport, activity? You will learn more and he will not feel as if he is being interrogated. As Johnny responds, you can tailor your discussion to fill him in on your home, how it operates, and make those accommodations you can to ease his transition.

Many of the young people in substitute care have been trauma victims. Any young person coming into a strange situation feels the uncomfortable sense of being the "new kid". With this in mind, there are a couple of very important inquiries you should make with Johnny.

One of the major issues you will want to broach with Johnny is how he handles things when he becomes frustrated, upset, sad, and/or angry. During your initial discussion or soon thereafter ask him, "Johnny, what really bothers you or gets you angry or frustrated?"

You might want to tell him about one of your minor triggers, "You know, Johnny, it irritates me when my co-workers don't flush the toilet at work. What bugs you?"

If he tells you something, thank him and acknowledge it. Then using yourself as an example you might say, "You know, when I get bugged at work I usually just take a few minutes by myself to calm down." Then you can pose the next question, "What works best for you when you are upset?"

If he gives you more information then you can lead into the final question by saying, "When I get frustrated I don't want anybody to talk to me, especially if it is the lady who hasn't flushed the toilet! Johnny, what do you want me to do or not do if I realize something seems to be bothering you?" This gives him a great opportunity to advise you how you should act.

If he tells you, "I need to be left alone," or "I need someone to talk with me right away," let him know that he is pretty smart if he knows what he needs when upset and that is how you will respond until he tells you different Please let the other folks living in the house know about this information so they, too, can respond accordingly.

If Johnny has little to say or does not join in the conversation, honor this silence. He will need time and space to figure out what is going on and try to adjust to a whole new world.

Following the "walking/talking tour," ask Johnny if he has further questions at this time. If not, clue him in on how the rest of the day will go, dinner, shower, study, bed times, etc. so he has a feel for what is coming up. This is a good time to suggest his taking care of personal business and settling in and offer assistance—possibly putting his clothing away in his room, getting him hygiene products so he can wash or shower, taking clothes to the laundry that need washing, homework, watching television, going outside, whatever. This gives him a chance to be alone if he so desires, or he can ask for your assistance.

It is important to give Johnny choices and options so that he is immediately making decisions for himself within parameters set by you. For example if dinner is at 6 PM, give him the option to do two or three things you know he needs to accomplish sometime that evening. Endorse what he chooses then provide direction for him to accomplish the others following dinner. Let's say Johnny wants to shoot baskets outside by himself for a little while, no problem. Let him know you will call him in a few minutes prior to dinner to wash up. Then, following dinner he will need to take care of homework, shower, whatever in a timely manner. You are establishing what he needs to do within the parameters that work for the family as a whole, but you are not dictating.

As you continue your first day with Johnny, plan on staying up until he has retired for the night. In fact, plan on staying up thirty minutes to an hour after he has gone to bed. Let him know you are doing so and will check in on him one last time before you call it a night.

This gives reassurance to him, and affords him a chance to talk without seeking you out. Remind him, prior to going to bed, about the morning routine and a little of what to expect the next day. Again... don't overload.

When you check on him for the last time, remind him where you are sleeping, location of the bathroom (leave a night light on in the bathroom), and how to get your help if needed. It is always good to affirm his being in your home with a brief statement of support, "Johnny, welcome aboard, I hope things work out for you soon, but you are welcome here."

Refrain from talking about being glad to have him or that you hope he is happy. Those are all feelings you and he might hold, but it is too early to voice them. If he is unhappy about being away from his family, how do you sound if you say you are glad?

The next morning you start all over again. Inquire how he slept, check for any problems or concerns, and talk a few minutes about the coming day. Discuss what is in store and how you all are going to proceed. If Johnny is to start at a new school, let him know your part in getting him enrolled or transferred. He'll need to know how books, lunch, fees and other initial expenses will be handled, as well as transportation. Then do as you said you would and provide the necessary support.

The first few days of placement will involve repetition, support, reassurance, checking in with Johnny, and dealing with everyone's adjustment and feelings. Open and honest communication is essential.

This is a major transition for any child. You can ease his transition by refraining from an "open house" for extended family members or neighbors. Introductions can take place over time, a few at a time as they naturally arise. Let him get acquainted first with you and your family.

Deal with the feelings expressed in a forthright manner and Johnny should be on his way to a less traumatic experience.

"The greatest good you can do for another is not just share your riches but to reveal to him his own."
-Benjamin Disraeli

I am not sure Disraeli's comment was made with young people in mind or as a tip for parenting. However, the point is valid and one of the "riches" we can reveal is the positive things our young people do. If you are observant and on the lookout for the "riches," you will not only see them but will help the child recognize such for himself.

Chapter 3

What can I do about Johnny's attitude? What does he think, and why does he think that way?

"There is nothing in a caterpillar that tells you it's going to be a butterfly." -Richard Buckminster Fuller

Johnny has a bad attitude, what can I do?

Jerry came slumping into the building after school trying with all his might to be invisible and slip past my office. He had to get past the door which faced the main hall leading to his dorm and the sanctuary of his room.

"Hey, Jerry", I hollered, with as much brightness as I could muster in my voice. This was a typical school day, and as his counselor, I tried to greet him and every youngster as they came home. I wanted to see how their day went and if there were any concerns, notes, field trip permits, etc. needing my attention.

As was Jerry's modus operandi, he tried to squirm by and shrink against the wall, often attempting to use another resident to serve as a "blocker" for him to get past my observation post and avoid what he saw as a negative interaction.

Today, Jerry was not so lucky. I had reason to be on the lookout for him, having received another phone call from his exasperated teacher in regard to his behavior, which she had characterized as "out of control!"

I did manage to get his attention, and with stooped shoulders he reluctantly dragged himself into my office and sat down, dropping his head, and staring at the floor. This had been our routine of late as school was not going well for this young man.

Jerry, a nice looking eleven year old young man, was having multiple problems controlling his temper and managing his anger. He had an especially difficult time in the classroom and toward his peers. He had enjoyed some success in both areas since coming to our agency, but school, even in special classes, was a struggle.

For the last week or so we started every afternoon on a negative foot due to a note from his teacher. School was a serious "downer" for Jerry, and I was quickly becoming another source of grief and contributed to his feelings of hopelessness and inadequacy.

We did manage to discuss the note and how he might choose to handle the situation in a more positive manner. Jerry was always quick to come to some kind of plan or agreement simply to get the hell out of my office, back to the dorm, and on to play where he could relax.

After our latest encounter, I knew something needed to change or we would lose what we had already gained with Jerry. I was also concerned that he would see us, me especially, not as helpful adults but just more people hassling him. His life had been full of hassles, from his mother, father, and various step parents he and his brother had lived with on and off for the last nine years. He came to our agency due to physical abuse by the last boyfriend living in his mother's home. I resolved to do something and felt the only people that might facilitate a change would be the teacher and me.

The next day, I called his teacher to discuss Jerry's latest problem on the playground. I listened to her tirade about Jerry's attitude being "horrendous," and that he was oppositional, defiant, surly, and angry. My response was, "Mrs. Smith, I recognize Jerry is struggling in school. What we are doing is not working, would you agree?" She did, and that set the trap for my wild suggestion.

"OK, we aren't getting anywhere so let's fool Jerry and change tactics. Let's do this for one week and see if we notice a difference in his behavior." I snuck in that "B" word as opposed to the "A" word to set the tone in her mind. Good old Mrs. Smith bit the baited hook and asked, "What might work for Jerry?"

My proposal was easy to implement if she would simply agree to start every note she sent home with a positive about Jerry. I wanted one positive comment in the first sentence so I could utilize it to focus Jerry on how he was behaving in an appropriate manner. Mrs. Smith, who was now hip to my ploy, said, "But he does nothing positive all day!"

I inquired if this was the case at lunch and recess, and she agreed those two periods were tolerable. I then requested she hone in on those two periods to find something the poor boy had done right and write about it to me that day. I then gave her license to carry on in the remainder of the note with the negatives. I heard a very disgusted sigh escape her, and possibly it was just a deep breath over my being an idiot in proposing such madness, but she did agree to try this for one week. I agreed that if she saw no improvement, she could feel free to go back to her daily diatribes about Jerry being an eleven-year-old terror.

That afternoon I waited for Jerry to come home. I admit being very anxious, in fact down right nervous that my proposal would not have as quick an impact as I had projected to Mrs. Smith.

Jerry, per usual, had the note in his hand. Not knowing it had a positive comment, he came through the door looking for a "blocker" to navigate the gauntlet that the hall had become since the start of school.

I did not give him the chance, immediately saying, "Good afternoon, Jerry (with a big smile), let me see that good note I heard about!" Jerry looked puzzled, and I think he thought I was being sarcastic as he handed over the envelope. I quickly read the first couple of sentences, something to the effect that, "Jerry did not fight or throw food today at lunch or at recess." Jerry looked at me with amazement, came around my desk and tried to read the note over my shoulder. I had hidden the bottom part with another paper, so all he could see were the positive statements.

Those two lines allowed us to focus on positives; the first positives in his school behavior for the last two weeks! As we discussed these improvements, we were able to talk about how he could go from decent behavior for part of the day to building decent behavior for more periods. He actually picked out times in the school day he felt he had a better chance of being successful, and we were able to come up with simple strategies.

Jerry was eager to try these strategies although somewhat unsure as to whether they would work completely. As I told him, "Some success is better than the same old failure," and he agreed to try.

Jerry's strategies (as they were mostly his plans with a few refinements thrown in by me) worked well the next couple of days, and he was excited. As I thought, the notes from school were remarkably more positive, and pointed out Jerry's improvements. His teacher called me after a couple of weeks of smooth sailing and stated she did not know what I had done, but Jerry's "attitude" had improved considerably. I deflected her compliment to me and shifted the congratulations on to

Jerry first, then thanked her for the recent change in the notes in which she tried to accent his positive behavior as much as possible.

We were able to take the good behavior exhibited at lunch and recess, build on it, and carry it over more and more. Because we started with classes Jerry liked, with allowing him to wait in the hall before school, etc., he was, in turn, more willing to try to control his behavior. The better effort he made to play his "bad hand of cards," the more positive reception from the teacher, which was reflected in the notes, which led to more improvements on Jerry's part.

Rather than have a cycle of self-defeating behavior perpetuated by negative reinforcement, we were able to start the cycle of positive behavior met with positive reinforcement, leading to more appropriate behavior. This was a perfect example of success breeding success.

As in the case of any child, poor behavior has to be supplanted with new behavior, hopefully more appropriate. To get the new and improved Jerry we had to break the steps down into small increments he could handle, rather than expect or demand a radical all or nothing transformation.

It has been my experience that utilizing nefarious adult terms like "attitude" does not help the child begin this process. It is the most overused word by adults toward children (except for "don't" and "stop"), and is misunderstood or taken in a negative context by children. When we as adults start in on a child regarding his "attitude" being poor, trust me, the child quickly tunes us out and hears, "Blah, blah, blah... you ain't doing what I think you should." The child gets the message that something is not right, and that something happens to be him.

Simply addressing attitude gives a child no clue what to change or improve. My guess is that most adults really don't understand the meaning of the word either. They also struggle when it is their attitude being addressed.

Asking Johnny to "lose" or change his attitude is like asking him to change the weather; he does not know how. Do yourself and Johnny a big favor, drop the word from your vocabulary and conversations, it is only confusing the real issue and clarifying nothing.

Rather than using "attitude," think behavior—the specific behavior that led you to believe the child has a bad attitude. Is it his words, his expression, tone of voice, body language, his response? If you can be specific and point the behavior out that you feel needs changing, the child then can make a choice as to a new behavior. Attitudes never change until we see a change in behavior. When someone changes the behavior, we think he has an improved attitude, and it is possible he does. However, the focus needs to be on the behavior being displayed which is causing you concern.

Everyone has the right to feel and think any way they so desire. Feelings and thoughts might reflect attitude, but how a person acts, his behavior, is what can be changed even if the thoughts and feelings remain the same. When we help a child change or improve a behavior, he learns how to change other behaviors. He can go, with your help, from a specific behavior to a generalization as to how to change.

"Life is not so much a matter of holding good cards, but sometimes playing a poor hand well."
-Robert Louis Stevenson

Think of your own poor habits you have broken or altered, be it diet, smoking, etc. As you learned to change one negative behavior, you also learned a methodology of how to change other behaviors or habits. The same holds true with children, although a child will have a slower process and will need our leadership, assistance, direction, modeling, and support.

His accomplishments need to be pointed out, given positive reinforcement, and all while you help him figure out the next step in the process. This process and these issues are not only germane to children in out of home care. Challenges with attitude seem to be a problem many parents are reporting.

I was approached a few years ago by a parent of a young man who was concerned about his son's negative "attitude" on the basketball court. The boy was a decent player, he had talent. But after watching him play in a tournament game, I could see why his father was concerned. In the game I observed Tim was assessed two technical fouls which in turn sent the opposing team to the foul line for the winning free throws. Tim had become angry over a call and had choice words with the referee and simply would not give up the issue until whistled the second time and was suspended from the game. His father was very upset, as were his coaches, other parents, and fans.

His father knew that I worked with children who had problems, including "anger management," and he approached me as to what he could do. As I normally do when asked for my "professional opinion" outside of the work place, I cautioned him that first I would need his honest assessment before weighing in with mine. I also advised that my opinion could still be sought if he so desired, but he would need to be prepared as it might not be what he would like to hear. This particular father was so upset with his son's antics he was willing to listen to anyone who might help, and he was forthright in his comments. He felt his son was playing out of control, losing the respect of teammates and other parents as well as the confidence of his coaches. Tim, he felt, was "hardheaded" and basically "uncoachable." He felt his "attitude" was horrible and needed a major change.

I first affirmed his concerns as being genuine. Tim was out of control, but my guess was his behavior on the basketball court was just the tip of the iceberg. His father agreed that Tim was struggling in school, and there were numerous arguments in the home. My second comment was to forget about Tim's attitude for now.

He was amazed to hear this as everyone else felt that attitude was Tim's major problem, including one of his coaches who had also spoken with me. It was my opinion that attitude was not Tim's problem; it was his behavior. I explained that attitude is really what you think and feel, and everyone has the right to think and feel as they so choose. However, where Tim was struggling was letting his feelings and thoughts come raging out in his behavior. Tim's feelings and thoughts about the referee did not cause the technical fouls; it was how he chose to behave on those negative thoughts and feelings that led to the referee's reaction.

I asked Tim's father what his son's response in the past was when he had discussed his attitude. He was honest in his reply stating, "Gary, Tim says he does not have an attitude problem." This came as no surprise to me. I then turned the discussion to Tim's behavior and how we might work with Tim on a few things he was doing on the court that had led to his recent difficulties.

It really helped to have video tapes of the games which we, Tim's dad and I, were able to look at, and later reviewed with Tim. We were able to point out his behavior, scowling, throwing a ball into the bleachers, threatening body space/language issues with the referee, pushing and taunting of other players, etc. These were concrete actions Tim could not deny because as the old saying goes, "the camera never blinks." The review was eye opening to both dad and his son, and we were able to talk with Tim as to how he might act if he could replay the various scenarios.

It is important to remember that children are video oriented. When we can use such techniques and the terminology they are using we have a better chance of connecting.

With Tim, we asked him to "punch the pause button," the idea to get him to stop and think briefly. I then asked him to "punch the rewind button," because he was going to get a chance to rework the scenario. Then I asked him to come up with one other possible reaction that was more positive than the one he had just witnessed.

My idea was to get Tim to think about his own buttons and how he has the power to "pause" or "stop action" and to "fast forward" to what things might actually happen. All of these are measures of self-control which we use to gain mastery over radical feelings and thoughts about those feelings.

I must admit, Tim was skeptical but agreed to try asserting better self-control as the alternative was more poor games. We concentrated on language, i.e. cussing on the floor, which drew attention to him, and space issues. If upset, he was not to go towards the official, but towards his bench where his coaches could help. Just those two things helped him throughout the remainder of the games in that particular tournament.

Lo and behold, people started talking about his improved attitude on the court. After a couple of games, Tim's dad met with me and actually wept. He informed me that no one had ever suggested approaching Tim in this manner. He also told me that Tim's mother was known for her attitude and when anyone tried to talk about Tim's, she took offense.

The problem with sustaining progress in situations like Tim's is getting everyone on board, other family members, coaches, etc. Unfortunately, Tim's mother never engaged in this process and enabled the poor behavior throughout his high school career, which, by the way, included three schools and four coaches.

I am not arguing to ignore feelings and thoughts, quite the contrary. I am simply stating that if you want change work on something that can be seen to change and is verifiable. There is nothing wrong with discussing feelings and thoughts that lead to behavior. In fact, this is an important part of the whole process. Our feelings and thoughts directly affect our behavior, but changing such is almost impossible without first influencing the behavior.

As I told Tim, to his father's amazement, "Tim I don't care if you want to kill the ref at the next game. I don't care if you want to call him everything in the book except for sir! But I do care how you look at him, how much space you put between the two of you, and that you bite your tongue until you are sure he can't hear you. Those are the three things I want you to focus on during the next game."

As Tim controlled the behaviors, my hope was that he would learn from the reinforcement that he need not act out on all feelings and thoughts. The reinforcers that I hoped would come into play were remaining in the game, being viewed by teammates as a reliable team member, winning the confidence of his coaches, and fewer issues with officials.

To tell Johnny, like Tim, not to think or feel is ludicrous in all matters. Since no one CANNOT think and feel, why then should he listen to you after receiving that advice?

There have also been occasions when I found it necessary to help a child learn how to "fake an attitude". I am sure many of you are thinking, "Fake it? What kind of counselor is this idiot? We should teach kids honesty and sincerity!" Hold that thought for a page or two.

One young man, Liam had a very strained relationship with his father. Dad was everything Liam was not and Liam was everything his dad could not or would not tolerate. Dad was a macho man, as the old song goes, "a hard drinking truck driving man." Liam was very laid back. His pursuits and interests were not fishing, hunting, driving trucks, or drinking.

To facilitate their being together to discuss important family issues, I knew very quickly that dad was not changing his ways, nor was he willing to meet Liam halfway. If there was going to be reconciliation, or at least peaceful coexistence, something had to give.

So Liam and I would role play his visits with dad. A big part of the act was Liam showing interest in what his dad had been doing of late. Liam got pretty good at this acting role. With time, he and his dad could actually meet and talk for an hour without my intervention or supervision. Dad was amazed at the new "attitude" Liam was demonstrating, and started behaving differently towards his son, actually using part of the time together to discuss Liam's concerns and interests. Dad's new interest in Liam was greatly appreciated by Liam and their relationship improved.

Finally, when we thought dad could stand the news, we confessed our role plays and dad was surprised to say the least. Liam's feelings and thoughts had changed very little but his behavior towards his dad led to his dad changing his behavior towards Liam. They actually found common interests—music and airplane models to mention two.

Liam's dad was a little upset with me, that I would teach a child to "fake" an attitude. His dad had been in the service so I used this as an example and asked if he had ever faked respect to an officer he could not tolerate. The look on his face indicated he had done so and that the light switch had hit the "on" position in his head. We were also able to discuss how their relationship had genuinely grown through this process and showed signs of stability and mutual respect.

"If there is anything we wish to change in the child, we should first examine it and see whether it is not something that could better be changed in ourselves."
-Carl Jung

Of course we want genuine interactions, but there are occasions when teaching the skill of "faking it" can be of major import to a child. It is, after all, a coping skill that can buy us time to think, reconsider, and then act more appropriately.

We all do this from time to time, probably more often as adults than we did as children. We fake enthusiasm, we fake laughter, we fake disbelief, we fake at times to cover our true feelings and thoughts, and we fake respect. Of course we tell ourselves our motives for such are good. And, they very well may be, as being "genuine and candid" would serve no good purpose.

An example... you get pulled over for speeding, you're going just ten miles per hour over the limit and fifteen cars have passed you by in the last two minutes. The police, however, pulled you over and your thoughts and feelings are most likely not thankful or kindly disposed to the trooper. In my case the thoughts are, "Why me, idiot? Didn't you see those other folks? Geez this pisses me off!"

But when that officer approaches my window I am already taking out my license and registration and reminding myself to be respectful. Acting on my "genuine and sincere" feelings and thoughts will probably not help the situation. I fake an "attitude" of respect and compliance.

This "faking it" is a skill that Johnny can utilize in many situations— at school, in the community, etc. He may not "genuinely" like his English teacher, but he can respond in a manner that indicates a respect for the position of the teacher, if not the person. You can help him in this endeavor by role playing for his next encounter.

I have conducted numerous skills group activities for children, especially adolescents. One I repeatedly offer is, "The A word: your attitude sucks!" I first ask if anyone in the group knows the meaning of attitude. Almost all have an opinion as to what an attitude is. When I ask, "OK, how can you change an attitude?" The response is silence.

After a review of much of the above I distribute the following hand out to give each participant something tangible for reference.

IT'S ALL IN HOW YOU...

A – act

T – think

T – talk to yourself

I – it's your choice how you live your life

T – talk to others

U – use coping skills

D – decisions and choices

E – express feelings

or…

A – approach people/problems

T – tolerate differences

T – talk with others

I – "I'm" responsible for myself

T – tone of voice

U – use language, smile, and be pleasant

D – disagree with others

E – effort and enthusiasm

"We become what we tell ourselves we are."
-Mary Pipher

The purpose of the group and worksheet on "Attitude," is to give young people something they can reference and call upon when adults start using the "A" word.

I have also provided parents with the worksheet so they can think of other ways to convey to their adolescent what they mean when they talk about "attitude." The idea is that instead of talking about "attitude," the parent begins the discussion talking about acts, decisions, thinking, choices, expressions, etc.

I like Mary Pipher's comment, "We become what we tell ourselves we are." I would add this addendum... young people often become what WE tell them they are!

Please remember... not all of our children have the wherewithal—intellect, maturity, vocabulary, etc. to make the choices we would like them to make.

This is especially true of children who have experienced trauma. Their brains and psyche have often been damaged from the emotional, psychological, and physical abuse they have suffered. Therefore, our expectations cannot exceed what their capabilities are. Trauma not only plays an important role in shaping what kids think, but also how they think, and therefore how they act.

It is very likely if you are in the "'substitute role" you are parenting a child who has experienced trauma. Your child has most likely encountered one traumatic episode—like Humpty Dumpty—he, too, has been pushed or fell from the wall.

A good rule of thumb, and one we reinforce with our staff, is to treat each young person you work with as a child who has experienced sexual abuse or trauma.

Some of the characteristics of the thinking process of trauma victims are:

Memory loss

Focus on survival needs – Johnny is going to spend more time thinking about his next meal than on a Geometry question.

Decreased ability to process verbal messages

Messages and meaning of such are processed by facial expression, tone of voice, body language

And in some cases, mostly with children who have been traumatized repeatedly, the child may "zone out," and appear to withdraw from the conversation and the thinking process. Psychiatrists call this disconnect a "dissociative state."

Therefore when you are engaged with a youngster who has been a trauma victim, keep this in YOUR mind when you are wondering what is going on in HIS mind.

As to young people in general, you are also going to notice major changes in a child as they reach adolescence, which some experts believe is closer to age eleven and twelve years than the thirteen or fourteen years which has been the general consensus.

When our kids cross that border and inhabit the land of adolescence, it seems WE ALL BECOME SUBSTITUTE PARENTS!!

I can remember the year I crossed into that world of adolescence and my mother commenting on the major changes she was seeing and feeling. Her exact words to me one summer evening were, "What happened to the Gary I knew that lived here last summer?" I felt and thought I was the same person, but she was seeing a uniquely different young man.

It is a kind of "invasion of the mind snatchers", that we, parents and young people alike, experience at the onset of adolescence.

If Men are from Mars, and Women are from Venus... what planet did these kids come from?!?

Some of you may remember, as I, the best seller from 1992, *Men are From Mars and Women are from Venus*, written by John Gray. His book looked at the "differences" between men and women above and beyond the physical/sexual features and attributes. Mr. Gray tackled the differences in thinking, perspective, perception, etc. and how such influenced behavior.

I am not a neuroscientist or researcher but if you think kids think different than you, so do I. And guess what... you are right.

There are many differences between the mature adult and adolescents. Each day we are learning more and more about how we work and what makes us "tick" physiological, psychological, sociological, and neurological.

In the world of the brain, neurological research has doubled in data and knowledge in the last twenty years. It is estimated by scientists that scientific knowledge doubles in two years or less. There is a wealth of information accessible to all of us about our bodies, brains, psychosocial well-being, etc. with neurological data being empirically based rather than theory. We can thank or curse, depending upon your view, the M.R.I. and increased technology, for increasing our knowledge base, especially with images of the brain.

Adolescent brain development has benefited tremendously from this research and it is really in its infant stage... no pun intended.

However, before delving into the "teen brain" we need to look at basic adolescent development as it all ties together in our kids. First and foremost, we need to recognize that.

But take heart, do not be afraid. For if we have understanding of these "spirits" we can engage, encourage, and with our efforts help them to excel. There is nothing easy in being an adolescent, it is a time of tremendous change when the person is least equipped for such change.

Adolescence is a stage of development unique to the human species.

Therefore, unlike cancer, heart disease, and other physiological maladies, we have not been able to use animals to look at their "adolescent brains." Unfortunately, Mickey and Minnie Mouse skipped that developmental stage.

But, the good news is... Most of us, having gone through the experience, are familiar with the apparent physical changes, rapid growth spurts, onset of puberty, secondary sex characteristics (hair, breast development, acne). Most of these come with some degree of discomfort and difficulty for the teen or pre-teen.

But, the bad news is... We tend to forget our struggles as a teen and lose sight of other factors such as:

PSYCHOSOCIAL FACTORS:
There are also changes to their psychosocial self. They become preoccupied with their image and how that "fits" into their self-perception.

It is a time for trying on many roles, joining groups or cliques, fads in clothes, music, etc.

Being popular is of paramount importance, even to the few who claim the contrary.

If not the popular trend setter, the teen tends to follow the popular or charismatic peer... all the while searching for their own unique identity.

They spend less time at home engaged with family, especially parents. Friends are what count.

There is the "push/pull" struggle for independence from the parent or substitute parent.

Feelings are up and down as well as ambivalent. The need for privacy is important. Behaviors at this time of life can seem, to us adults, as risky, thrill seeking, irrational, purposeless, and immature.

INTELLECTUAL FACTORS:

This is a time when the young person will develop abstract thinking but can go back and forth from abstract to concrete, which tends to drive us adults a little nutty.

Sometimes there will be great clarity where all seems to be running a smooth course and LOGIC and REASONING are being utilized.

Problem solving usually involves a step by step process of looking at and eliminating obvious choices.

This can be the time when the young person starts thinking a little more deeply, especially as to values, but it is more often characterized by the rejection of adult and parent values.

We will see a great reluctance to admit a lack of knowledge or to being wrong. Teens seldom let the cold hard facts interfere with their opinions, especially when it is the adult delivering the cold hard facts.

So what are we to do? First let me caution what not to do.

Do not give adult motivations to a child/teen's behavior!!

It is such an easy trap to fall into, and we drag the kid in with us, when we think we know what he is thinking and why he is thinking, feeling, acting this way, based upon what our motivations would be.

We have mature adult brains to think with, our kids do not. This is not theory, it is biological fact. As previously stated, we are a heck of a lot smarter about our kids and their brains than ever before. What some of us guessed was true is true—kid's brains are different than ours.

We now know, and are learning more at an astronomical rate, that a teen's brain is a "work in progress." According to a multitude of research projects and studies starting around the age of eleven or twelve years old on up into the early twenties, Johnny's brain is developing much like his body—changing and adapting.

We are all aware of the tremendous HORMONAL impact on our kids, especially the sexual hormones—testosterone and estrogen. We can see the physical manifestations, or at least quite a few with our eyes.

But there are more below the surface and very actively involved in Johnny's brain, Sarah's, too.

The "brain" under stress, yours and mine, produces a negative chemical "cortisol," that can cause a lack of memory, depressed or angry mood, and a definite loss in mental alertness. A fully matured "adult brain" is better equipped to respond and function than that of a child or teen.

When fear is aroused, our brains secrete an overabundance of the chemical adrenaline, and can result in decreasing our ability to make good decisions. Again the teen brain is less equipped in the "decision" making area of the brain than the adult and therefore more apt to make poorer decisions. This can be fear from external sources or simply the fear of uncertainty, and we all recognize adolescence is a time of great uncertainty.

The good news is that we can help our kids get a boost of a more positive brain chemical, dopamine, which acts much like an anti-depressant, making him, and for that matter us, feel better. M.R.I. studies and research show that such a chemical boost can be initiated when a teen receives praise, feels he has been treated fairly, and given respect.

Empirical evidence now supports our theories that neurological development can be greatly influenced by many factors:

Genes, Infections, Injury, Nutrition (pre- and post-natal) as well as social circumstance such as child abuse and social pain. The social pain of being rejected, berated, over-criticized can have the same impact on the brain as actual physical pain.

How many teens feel rejected? Berated? Inadequate? Over criticized? Adolescence is a time of life where we are extremely alert to rejection and take most things very personal. The adolescent brain feels this pain and is impacted by such in a negative manner. It is also apparent that negative thoughts and deeds tend to breed more of the same. The brain changes based on where or on what the teen pays attention to... what Johnny spends his time doing becomes "wired" into his brain. This is a major concern to those of us who are working or living with teens that use substances.

Drugs, Alcohol, and Nicotine can have negative impact on the brain and the effects can be permanent!!!!

Unfortunately, another area in which Johnny's brain differs from ours is the susceptibility to the various addictions—be it drugs, alcohol, nicotine, the internet and all of its information. Whereas the adult brain can fight off some of the lure and thrills of such addictive items, his brain is not as equipped to do so.

Johnny will use different parts of his brain than we do in responding to the same tasks and stimuli.

The good news as to his brain (as compared to ours) is his brain is actually over producing "gray matter" during his adolescence, ours as adults is not productive in that manner. The bad news is his production can be seriously impeded and damaged with such things as alcohol, drugs, and other stimuli. There is research coming out as to one of those addictions being our computers, cell phones, and over use of our gadgets... our kids are hard wiring themselves to distraction and their ability to focus is being harmed. Sometimes people refer to this distraction addiction as multi-tasking, but I tend to believe it is, with teens, more of a case of multi-distracting.

No doubt Johnny's brain as it develops and produces more gray matter through adolescence triggers his desire to learn, and learning is exciting (I said learning, not necessarily education). However, we also know he tunes out and turns off quicker than we do, and his attention span and focus are not commensurate with the adult brain.

With this in mind, learning of any kind needs to be broken down to teen size nuggets that his brain can digest; small increments and as much hands on as possible, rather than in adult size portions and our methods.

Johnny's brain is less responsive to logic than ours and he relies upon his senses to understand what is going on, more so than logical thinking. Therefore, he is more likely to get his messages and interpret such through his "reading" an adult's face, tone of voice, body language, and emotions.

Let's take a cursory look at the brain.

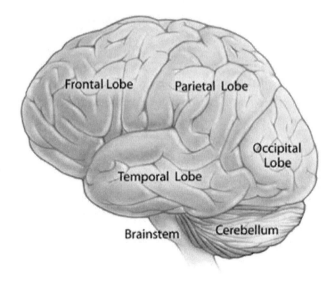

As stated before I am not a neurologist or a psychiatrist, but a basic explanation of these parts of the brain is as follows:

The occipital lobe's major function is vision.

The temporal lobes have a lot to do with emotional maturity and we know those lobes are still maturing past the age of sixteen. The temporal lobes also have the most to do with memory, language, hearing, and emotions.

The parietal lobes are used to integrate and process messages received from our senses. The parietal lobes make sense of the various messages or signals we get by our vision, hearing, and touch. These, like the temporal, are still immature past the age of sixteen.

I want to concentrate on the frontal lobes as this is the most critical area of difference between teens and adults.

The frontal lobes are very interesting in the differences between Johnny and us. Understanding "how" he thinks is more important than understanding "what" he thinks.

The frontal lobes have a lot to do with "how" he thinks.

This is the part of his brain where we see the most changes. It is also the area of the most growth.

The frontal lobes are not mature until early adulthood, somewhere between the ages of 20 and 23 years. These lobes have the most to do with our self-control, executive decisions, cognition, judgment, organization, insight, and regulating our behavior.

For the most part, Johnny uses a different part of his brain to regulate emotions, his amygdala (a small part of his temporal lobes), and responds based on his fears and gut feelings more so than logic and reason. Utilization of this part of the brain to process may lead to mistakes, and a rewarding of things that FEEL rewarding to him. Social rewards from peers, especially, leads to more attention being paid to the social reward. This can lead to what we see as risky behavior or sensation seeking, with an emphasis on the rewards and little regard given to the consequences. His control center, his frontal lobes, are just not mature, everything is not totally connected, and are therefore more sluggish and less capable of performing as they do once he has brain matured.

Another area deserves mention, too, due to the significant difference in the adolescent as compared to the adult. This area, which actually connects the two hemispheres of the brain, is the corpus callosum, which is involved in self-awareness, intelligence, and consciousness. It appears this part of the brain is not fully mature until Johnny is twenty years old or older.

The purpose of this brief discourse is to get us to think and recognize differences. We may be asking teens to do some things they cannot do as well as we would expect. It is not necessarily because they are oppositional or that their thinking is truly distorted, they are simply not as well equipped as most of us adults.

So, now that I know a little bit more about Johnny's brain and thinking, what can I do to help?

The real experts in the field of neurology say there are a lot of things we can do that impact thinking (adult and teen) as well as improving brain function.

Some of these experts estimate that most of us use between 3% to 5% of our brains. I have read other opinions that it can be as high as 10% to 15%. But when engaged in a learning experience that involved our excitement and coupled with a physical activity (hands on) we can grow' that use up to a level as high as 90%.

With young people, active teaching, coaching, demonstrating, and modeling will stimulate more so than being told or lectured on what to do.

Brains do not grow when told what to do; brains grow, build connections, and learn new skills by being involved in the learning process.

Have you ever asked yourself why your teen seems to want to sleep twelve hours? I have, especially when my son was in high school and playing sports. He could sleep fourteen hours without stirring on a weekend or holiday.

The answer is simple and somehow complex... the simple, sleep helps. The complex, sleep is when teens integrate learning into long term memory. Educational experts strongly suggest young people refrain from pulling all night study sessions and instead study for short periods of time, then sleep on it. How many of us have come up with better solutions to seemingly insolvable problems after a good night's sleep.

Nutrition is important. Good food in means good brain results out. Garbage in results in garbage out... and the toxic garbage such as alcohol, drugs, and nicotine is, of course, the worst.

Encourage physical activity and the bringing in of good oxygen from exercise. Getting your teen involved in a brief exercise stimulates the brain and releases positive natural chemicals that help him think in a more positive, clear fashion.

Stay involved with your teen. Your involvement and interest stimulates him as well as you. Stay active with him, listen, talk, explore ideas, and engage in physical exercise and work with him. Some of the best times I remember sharing with my father were while we were doing manual labor. While we worked we had to collaborate and cooperate, sharing the tasks, setting the goals, and earning the same rewards. All of these are skills we so desperately want our kids to incorporate into their lives. One of my father's favorite sayings before we would start a project was, "Gary, if you don't learn how to work by age ten, you never will." I did not understand or agree with that statement then, but I did by the time my children came along at age 25.

Involve your child in problem solving, explaining procedures, objectives, goals, and possible outcomes and start this the first day the child enters your realm.

Set clear expectations. Brain research supports that children do better and develop in a more positive manner when the adults involved in their lives are "warm, but firm; open and fair" setting clear expectations, rewards and consequences. You can do so in an authoritative way without being dictatorial and they can wire these behaviors into their brains and use in the future.

Recognize and respond to both the positive and negative behaviors. Deal not only with the behavior but the reasons, purposes, and thinking behind such. Accept failure when your child is trying a new task, be ready for setbacks and repeated errors, encourage, engage, and model what you want to see.

Listen then bite your tongue and listen again. I have found it a good practice both in my work and with my own children, to remind myself to ignore the first words out of a teen's mouth, as such are usually not thought out. Their thoughts, pushed by their feelings, can gush out. Given a few seconds to utilize their frontal lobes, the second offering can be much easier to accept and understand.

Allow for expressions of fears, anxieties, hopes, dreams, worries and all of the emotions. Kids feel them so intensely and we can only hope to help them sort through these things by respecting those feelings. A fourteen year old in love is every bit as much in love, and probably more intensely, that a forty year old in love.

Tell the truth, answer questions with honesty. Admit you can be wrong and apologize as needed.

I saw a sign in a church yard the other day and it speaks volumes, *"Practice what you preach; better yet, forget the preaching, just practice!"*

Parenting and especially "substitute" parenting takes a lot of practice.

Chapter 4
Why does Johnny behave like this? What can I do to help?

"If nothing ever changed there'd be no butterflies."

When I returned to our agency in the summer of 1988 we operated two basic programs—residential treatment and emergency shelter care.

The shelter could be used by law enforcement personnel (police/sheriff), the local juvenile courts, and child protective service of the local departments of child welfare and services for temporary care of children ages six to eighteen years. At that time a child could be placed in emergency shelter care for 72 hours while the affected agency conducted its investigation into family and/or legal issues.

Prior to leaving campus each evening I would stop by the shelter—a separate building from our residential dorms. It was just a habit I developed as I wanted to check on any new youngster placed, make sure they had what they needed, as well as check in with the one staff member who provided the supervision.

The shelter was arranged very much like a home and our meals were served family style at a large dining room table.

One particular evening upon checking I ran into a most unusual family dining experience. Four brothers had been placed earlier that same day and were not happy about the change in their lives.

I decided to join them at the table. Following a brief prayer by Ms. Baylor, our 22 year old staff member, all hell broke loose with the brothers elbowing and grabbing for food, which quickly escalated into an all-out fight.

After the initial shock, we both jumped into the fracas to restore order and were able to separate the warring parties. Within a few minutes all of us were seated back at the table. Before starting to eat, I wanted to talk about what had just happened.

Neither Ms. Baylor nor I could figure out what had led to the "donnybrook at dinner time." So I simply asked the boys, "What in the hell just happened here, guys?" The oldest brother, Will, stated, "That's how we settle who gets the chicken breast." His response was very matter of fact and his expression was one of nonchalance, with a mix of befuddlement that I did not understand this family custom.

After a moment of astonishment I told the boys that it was not necessary to fight over food or anything else, we had plenty to go around and no one would be left hungry. It would have been pointless and counterproductive to have belittled or criticized their behavior as it was the way they handled and approached such issues. I simply wanted to get their attention and let them know such behavior was not necessary in our facility for any reason.

I did not condemn or condone their behavior but wanted them to consider ways to behave so that all of them got what was needed without anyone being harmed or going hungry. To their credit, these boys were not particularly mean spirited or wanting to cause harm to one another. In fact, they proved to be a close knit group and extremely loyal. They each wanted to eat, to get the most the quickest so they would be full, something quite rare in their lives. Prior to placement they had operated on the premise, "to the victor goes the spoils," in this case the chicken breast.

We chose not to belabor what they were used to doing in their family, or how such behavior was unusual. We chose instead to recognize where they were coming from and to build improved skills so they would learn how to get their needs met in a healthy manner. We assured them that although they might not always get what they WANT, we would guarantee they would get what they NEED.

Children like these brothers and their families present real challenges to us in our substitute parental role and it is crucial we keep our focus on the behavior exhibited and the dynamics behind the actions.

Behavior, unlike Attitude-Thoughts-Feelings-Motivations, can be seen. Behavior can be described, demonstrated, and modified. We cannot "show" a child his thoughts, feelings, attitude, motivations. We can only guess and assume, which often leads us down the wrong path, escalating and alienating the child in the process.

We can, however, "play back behavior" and talk about what happened and how the child and others acted. It is important that we learn how to recognize and focus on behavior. Doing so allows us to engage the child without engendering negative perceptions of his persona, family, feelings, and thoughts of being under attack.

You need to recognize in yourself and to yourself that it is not always possible to "love" or at times even "like" a particular child and the behavior exhibited. At times we know very little about the child when he is tossed or placed in our care.

It helps to remember it is the child experiencing the trauma and disruption, much more so than us. We volunteered for our roles and the major changes and transitions are theirs with which to struggle and grapple.

Although "love" is hard to give and very often not wanted or acknowledged, we can offer and adopt the position of UNCONDITIONAL POSITIVE REGARD AND RESPECT. This is the belief, with actions congruent to the belief, that all people have value and our needs are similar. We share common wants, fears, feelings, and thoughts with most people, including the child in our care. Therefore each person, although unique, deserves our respect and regard.

"It is not genius, nor glory, nor love that reflects the greatness of the human soul; it is kindness."
-Henri Lacordaire

If your desire is to be effective in your substitute role, it is essential that your focus be on Johnny's needs, feelings, thoughts, and behaviors. All behavior has a purpose. However, not all behavior of a child has adult motivations or sophistication. It is easy to fall into the trap of believing Johnny behaves as he does for the same reason as an adult. It is also easy to fall into another trap with Johnny, to look at his behavior and see "underlying" maladjustment," due to his being in placement. What we might view as "typical" becomes "atypical" for a child in placement outside of his home.

One young man placed with us wet his bed one night. Being vigilant and wanting to do the right things, speculation started as to his possibly being a victim of child sexual abuse or some other such trauma. Now if that young man had been in my home or yours as a guest for a "sleepover," that thought would probably not cross our minds. The situation he was in led to our concerns more so than the actual behavior.

As to motivations, I could not give the "chicken breast" fighting brothers adult motivations for their unruly behavior at the dinner table. Why did they behave in such a manner? Because in their experience, such behavior worked and was most likely reinforced.

For the most part, like the brothers, we learn our behavior from our immediate role models... our parents and other family members. The family reinforces our behaviors sometimes in a positive manner and at times in a negative fashion.

"For behavior, men learn it, as they take diseases, one of another."
-Francis Bacon

Be prepared as changing behavior is going to cause discomfort, disruption, and often elicit strong emotional responses.

A variation of the old adage, "You can take the boy out of the country, but you can't take the country out of the boy," rings true for children and the ties to their families. "You can take the boy out of his family, but you can't take the family out of the boy."

With this in mind we need to look for strengths and positives within each child and his family. We can use these to start with the child and improve skills that are already present, just not as effective or developed as he may need.

One of my encounters as a child protective service caseworker speaks to both of the above statements.

I removed three young boys, ages five, seven, and nine from their parents after two investigations. Their father had been beating the boys across the back of their legs and buttocks with a thick belt, leaving welts. In fact, the police and I walked into the house when one such beating was taking place. This particular beating took place for inappropriate behavior at the dinner table, arguing with his brother. Mr. F. had administered other such belt beatings over school issues, backtalk to their mother, fighting with each other, etc. Concerns by the school bus driver who witnessed one of Mr. F.s beatings led to our investigation.

Mr. F. did love his children and they loved him. What he did he did, in his stated opinion, to "correct" and "discipline my boys." He did not view this as harmful, let alone abusive. The boys although not happy about being whipped, held no animosity towards their dad as they felt they "had it corning."

As we came to know each other during various discussions, he confided in me that he was incredulous that I removed his children from his care. He was willing to listen to my reasons, but this one comment of his revealed a lot.

His comment, with his voice rising and emotional was, "Gary, that ain't abuse! I know what abuse is! My daddy did it to me!" He was tearful during this revelation and as I listened he explained that his father had indeed hit with a 2 x 4 board on his back when he misbehaved. He peeled off his shirt to prove his point—he did have the scars.

As I worked with Mr. F. and his family, more abusive behavior came to light involving his father which was subsequently investigated. Mr. F. carried more than the physical scars on his back. As he went through the process of parenting classes and counseling, he too received some help and acquired new skills that did not involve hitting his children with a belt. His wife also did what she needed to do to get the boys returned to their care, and they were diligent in their efforts.

It helped that during the time out of their parents' home the boys were able to stay with family members and have ongoing and frequent contact with their parents. It was also helpful that the police and prosecutor, although upset at the time of their intervention, chose not to file criminal charges as long as Mr. and Mrs. F. followed the requirements of the Juvenile Court.

It took a few months but the boys were returned to their home. During my tenure as a child protective services worker we did not receive a report of further abuse. Mr. F. was doing what he thought was right, Mrs. F. agreed, as did the boys who throughout the ordeal refused to speak poorly of either parent and felt the "belt whippins" were warranted. In Mr. F.'s mind he was a good dad and conscientious—in his own way—not to repeat the mistakes of his father.

Had we, the police, and court only looked at the negatives in this family, I doubt the results would have been the same. Mr. F. most likely would be in jail, the boys in long term care, and the family shattered.

People not familiar or involved in the care and protection of children are stunned when they hear of such cases—usually upon the death of a child. They are also amazed when the child or children are then later returned to their families, usually the parent or parents from whom they were removed.

It is a fact of life, now more than ever, that children in the vast majority of cases are going back home. This does not mean they are going home without services or protective guidelines in place (although as we know these are not fail proof). Recent trends in family and child services have undergone a major shift to "family based in home services," and away from out of home care.

It is my opinion that each child needs to be looked at on a child by child basis and services delivered in the MOST APPROPRIATE and LEAST RESTRICTIVE placement, as close to home and community as possible.

If you are going to work in this field or provide care as a substitute parent (foster, relative or step), be aware of the above trend as the child in your care is temporary and most likely going home.

However, with that said, it has been my experience that efforts geared towards children and their families as a unit have the best overall results. Most children want to go home and do their best when involved, engaged, and attached to their families.

Recognizing this fact we, all of us who say we care for kids, need to put our efforts and resources into strengthening families—ALL KINDS OF FAMILIES. That is where children are being raised and learning their behavior that will be reflected throughout their lives and impacting our communities.

One of the main things to keep in mind is that the child in your care is in your care, usually, due to circumstances beyond his immediate control. Please do not forget this child may have experienced numerous traumatic incidents in his life. We need to play to his strengths. One that jumps out is resiliency. Focus on building his coping skills so he can adapt and move forward.

If we can approach these children from a "skills deficient" mind set, again focusing on strengths, we are more likely to have success or a chance of raising their skills to the optimal level of performance while in our care.

Children in out of home care have not learned, been exposed, or developed effective, rational, socially appropriate and/or healthy ways, means, and skills to cope with life, be successful in school, build relationships, and self-manage their emotions.

Remember, too, that these children, in some cases, have been exposed to the exact opposite. They may have witnessed over and over ineffective, irrational, unacceptable, and unhealthy means of coping, BUT do not recognize them as such. They often seem to be alright with those means and follow the pattern of behavior played out in front of them by their parents, families, and immediate communities. I would be considerably wealthier today if I had $1 for every child or family member who has exclaimed to me, "But you don't get it… that's the way we have always done it."

Many of the children we encounter are basically skill less. Those who do not do well are not doing it because they want to. THEY DON'T KNOW HOW. And, they do not know how to get the help needed to build those skills necessary to do well. This is also the case with many of their families.

"There is nothing that can be changed more completely than human nature when the job is taken in hand early enough."
-George Bernard Shaw

Mr. Shaw's comment is true, but the sword cuts both ways, positive as well as negative changes.

Common characteristics of children coming into residential or foster care placement include: physical, sexual, and emotional abuse or neglect. Very few children are placed outside of their homes for a poor home environment; this is handled by in home services. Truancy, substance abuse, and minor delinquent acts are other behaviors leading to placement. Other characteristics include grief and loss, developmental issues, and for lack of a better description, deficient development of "values" common to success within the community. We are also seeing a significant increase in "homeless" young people. This increase might be due to recent economic hard times as well as how "homeless" is now defined.

As to developmental issues, I am not just referring to autistic children or those suffering from a form of mental retardation. What I am referring to is most children who have to leave their home, be it for whatever reason, and I include divorce and step children, usually do not function at what we would consider appropriate age level.

Such trauma impacts overall function and a child of age fourteen might act like a child of twelve. The reverse can also be true as some of these young people have had "street experiences" of a twenty year old by the time they are thirteen. So it is not uncommon in our facility to see a fifteen year old, in some ways acts like he is twelve, and then in other ways exhibit behaviors of a young man age nineteen or twenty.

Chris, a boy of age twelve, is a prime example of the above issues. He was placed a few years back with us. He crossed the threshold angry, forlorn, hostile, decked out in leather, spike haircut, lighter, cigarettes, a knife, chains and motorcycle insignia (his mother was a member of a local "outlaw" club). He was loud, opinionated, and expressed himself with profanity that would make a hardened sailor blush.

At first we were at a loss as to what to make of Chris. At the time we had one dorm (six to eight boys on average) of younger boys ages eight to twelve, and an older boys dorm (eight to ten boys on average) ages thirteen to eighteen years. Not knowing which dorm was most appropriate, we started Chris on the older boy's dorm as he presented more like a sixteen year old than a ten year old.

Over the 4th of July, some of our young people went to a four day camp run by the local YMCA. They would camp, fish, swim, play games, hike, etc. We always transported both ways, made sure they were prepared and had what they needed, like any parent would. The kids seldom had any problems during their stay. The Y folks were great and knew if someone got sick or had a problem they could call us and we would respond. I received a call after the first day of camp involving Chris. I was requested to pick him up as soon as possible as he was no longer welcome. Apparently he had broken just about every rule for the campers within the first 24 hours.

I did pick him up and on the way back, about a 45 minute drive, he talked and I listened. His talk first centered on how unfair he had been treated at camp and that you "grown-ups are always out to F--- me." His talk then went into examples of how he had been "F'd" all of his life, and he was correct, he had been terribly mistreated. One thing became very evident—Chris had never been allowed to be a little boy. He did not speak about this with regret or "poor pitiful me" tone, it was matter of fact, and in a resigned manner.

I don't believe Chris was trying to excuse his behavior at camp (smoking and cursing) or to get me to understand why he acted as he did at camp. However, he did want me to understand under what conditions he had operated and could operate.

Chris had cultivated this "badass" persona, modeled by his mother's boyfriends, as he felt it ensured his physical and emotional safety. His physical appearance was his "armor," and his behavior exuded a "don't trespass on me" message which kept people at a distance. Therefore he was safe (he had been molested by one of his mother's friends).

One of the things I decided to do with input from our Recreational Director was to move him to the younger boy's dorm. This would give him contact, interaction, and experiences with a younger age group. We hoped this would also allow him to let down his defenses a little bit, decrease overall expectation from staff, provide a different peer "audience", and exposure to more age appropriate activities. With the older boys, Chris felt compelled to keep up his "badass" role and out "badass" the others.

The move to the younger boy's dorm, like any transition, had problems but there was also some success.

One day our Recreational Director asked me to walk outside without making a big deal of it and observe what was going on outside of Chris' dorm area. We had recently put in a large sandbox that could accommodate four to five kids. Many of our young people did not know what to do in a sandbox and it took our Recreational Director to show some "how to play." This included building tunnels, playing with cars, trucks, and various boys toys with which most of us are familiar. When I walked outside, there sat Chris, still decked out in his motorcycle vest, ear rings dangling, blue black hair spiked... playing with trucks and cars with two other boys.

It hit me again that day as to how many of our children have not been allowed to be children. In some of the worst cases, such as sexual abuse and molest, their childhood and innocence has been stolen.

Really, the word stolen seems too kind. Their childhood has been RIPPED from their hearts and thrown away in the trash!

I would like to report that Chris went on to be very successful in our facility, but he did not. He struggled in placement (primarily I believe because one of us was not able to penetrate that hardened veneer and establish a relationship), ran away a few times (rare for our facility) and was eventually returned to his mother's care. We lost contact with Chris soon thereafter and his mother had talked about returning to Texas where she had family.

I mentioned earlier what I called a "value deficiency." This is not meant to offend anyone, however it has been my observations over my career that a large number of children in out of homecare often UNDERVALUE what most of us know to be essential factors in living a fairly happy and successful life—family belonging, cohesiveness, independence, employment, ownership, education, to name a few.

By the time a young person is admitted to our facility, he is usually in trouble in school, behind two to five grade levels as to skills, and attendance has been sporadic. He has attended four to six schools in his career above and beyond the expected moves due to promotion, and experienced numerous behavioral problems including out of school suspensions and being expelled.

Family involvement with the school has been minimal so partnering with the family by the school just does not take place. Study skills, reading, preparing for school, getting to bed on time, getting up on time, doing homework, eating a balanced breakfast, accessing tutoring services, etc. are all relatively new developments in many of our kid's lives. We have to teach, reinforce, and reward our children as they get used to the new routines and acquire the necessary skills.

Two prime examples come to mind, and there have been hundreds quite similar.

The first young man, Banks, was one of my all-time favorite kids. He was twelve years old the second time he was placed with us (he had been in placement briefly when he was ten). He was smart, very capable of articulating his needs, thoughts, points of contention, view, etc. I admired his resiliency and courage, to say the least!

However, like many of the children I see capable of being self-assertive... he was not always diplomatic as he did so. When he came back to our program, he had already been expelled from his previous school while in the seventh grade.

We utilize our public schools and have been very fortunate as our local schools and school corporation work very closely with our program and the Court to keep kids, including ones like Banks, on track educationally and offer alternatives to your standard schools.

One of the things we wanted to tackle early on was coming up with a means of reinforcing decent and appropriate behavior and effort in school. We thought we could engage Banks and others in self-regulating their behavior with positive reinforcement that was tangible. If we could do so we thought he and our other young people had a better chance of learning than they did if suspended or expelled. Obviously you can't learn if you are not there.

Our #1 goal with Banks (and it is major focus goal for all of our residents) was to STAY IN SCHOOL... zero suspensions being the target. We decided if Banks and others would simply stay in school we would have a weekly reward of a school incentive coupon as part of our School Incentive Program. We also built in a monthly special activity reward for those students who remained in school the entire month without suspension. We geared the monthly reward to something educational in nature... a special notebook that was popular or extra money for a school field trip. Our coupon was a color coded picture of the Monopoly figure designed by our Recreational Director with the help of a couple of residents. Each school, initially, had a different color and was on board as to accepting these as "currency" in their bookstore. We would then reimburse the schools involved.

Obviously it took some work to get the schools to agree, but we found that the teachers and administration wanted these kids educated as much as we did. No one had come to them with an "outside" idea to encourage our residents. It is always easier to commit to such a program if you have a willing partner's support.

These coupons were distributed at the end of each week in front of everyone prior to dinner. We made a big deal out of this accomplishment. When Banks was approached on the School Incentive Store (SIP) and coupon, his first response was, "What a bunch of B.S." However, he never failed to be front and center when it was time to hand out the coupons or acknowledge papers and tests that received an A grade. He was obviously bright, but had lacked the challenge to let his light shine.

As with Banks, I truly believe that every young person I have known has a "light to shine," if allowed, and not snuffed out by us adults!

This program and incentive built a lot of unexpected excitement with our kids and they came up with all kinds of ideas as to the monthly activity (a Globetrotter game and a ride in a limo were two that I remember). Our schools liked the idea and were supportive, notifying teachers who in turn could discretely remind our students about the rewards.

The "buy in" from the residents was easy, less so with staff until they saw the results. Some felt we should not reward behavior that should be expected as the norm, others were concerned about possible embarrassment for the resident, although the resident had the choice to be involved.

Our response to any objection was we were going to try something rather than have a young person be kicked out and lay around all day in our dorms. If the incentive worked, with consequences also built in for those who were suspended, great, if not, we would scrap it and go on to something else. The SIP was so popular its first year that when presented to the local Junior League they became sponsors for the next school year and had a great time working with the residents on the monthly activity. (If by some chance I could locate those Junior League ladies today, I am willing to bet they feel they learned and got more out of our SIP than the residents involved).

Given a little time and positive results, our staff found that they, too, could use the coupon and SIP as reminders during tutoring and study times as well as getting up in the morning and off to school. Suspensions decreased dramatically and, as expected, school behavior was better. I was not sure the academics would indicate success due to the SIP, but over time grade improvement was a byproduct of attendance and improved behavior. Simply getting Banks and others to go and behave exposed them to the opportunity to learn.

Banks, as mentioned earlier, was not an easy "sale." At first he sat in class, did very little, faked bored indifference, but little by little he became engaged in the learning process, especially if the teacher was "engaging."

He started talking about what was going at school, things that interested him, extracurricular activities which we financed, school field trips, etc. The school personnel saw an immediate behavioral change (he was staying in class rather than spending the day with the principal) and in time his academics improved. By the end of the school year (in the 1980's and 1990's some of our residents remained in placement until school was out) he had earned the right to graduate and was promoted to high school.

As to the rewards/coupons, the day he left to go home I helped him clean out his room and pack his belongings. While going through his desk, I found most of the coupons he had earned in a neat stack. He had collected them, did not spend but the first few, and when I asked why, his response was, "Just wanted to see how many I could get." The coupons had lost their "face value" to Banks, what he valued most was what he was learning and accomplishing. Banks of course, true to his self, framed this a little different than I did, telling me, "I told you I would do it and those people could not kick me out this year."

What was sort of ironic with him was he was an avid fisherman, but I don't think he ever "got" that the "baited hook" of the SIP was thrown into his pond, but he bit… hook, line, and sinker.

The other young man I referred to was a fifteen year old named Ted. He was between his seventh and eighth grade year when placed with us, and obviously from his age and grade, his school performance to date had not been "stellar."

During the previous three school years he had attended seven different schools and had not, since the sixth grade made it through the entire school year. He was expelled (not an easy thing to do for any school corporation) in sixth and seventh grade. One of these expulsions was from an "alternative school" designed for students like Ted.

Ted was not stupid, although the loss of his skill base was a problem. Motivation was another issue to address, at least we thought so at the start.

However, the more we LISTENED to Ted the more he TAUGHT us... WE LEARNED that he and his family had moved at least ten times during that three year period, thus the ever changing school scene. WE LISTENED and LEARNED that he did not have clothes to go to school nor the means to pay book rental or for lunch, even at a reduced rate (at the time total free books and lunch were not available). WE LOOKED and RECOGNIZED that his one pair of shoes were rotten and falling apart. The odor was atrocious, and he was embarrassed.

One way for Ted to avoid embarrassment and humiliation in school was to act out, get kicked out (not a stigma in his family) and therefore avoid the hassles and humiliation. Many of us cannot imagine going to school in rotten shoes, the same clothes every day, and not being able to eat a school lunch when you are so hungry that it actually looks and smells good, regardless of the menu!

We started with the obvious... shoes and clothes, moved on to books and supplies, furnished a little money for the extra-curriculars (something he never was able to afford) and provided money for popcorn day weekly. Ted later confessed he always avoided going on popcorn day as it smelled so good and he did not have the money to buy it, nor did he want to answer the numerous questions as to why he was not getting popcorn like all of the rest.

How many of us would avoid school over the issue of 25 cents for popcorn? If it reminded us of what we did not have, could not have, while everyone else was getting it, my guess is a lot of us would find a way to avoid this humiliation on popcorn day.

We had to be careful with the clothes and shoes issue, and I caution you all to do the same. What looked and smelled horrible to me, were in Ted's perception his, and the last pair his mother had purchased for him. Smelly rotten shoes in my mind... Mom's last purchase for Ted in his mind. So I needed his permission as to how to handle his property. Did he want them thrown away at that time, or put outside to air out? He owned so very little. He chose to get rid of all of the items and we did so together.

We also enlisted the support of his new school and discussed prior issues and possible reasons, getting the school officials on board with their support. They were also used to working with our residents and had already bought in to the S.I.P.

Tutoring and incentives were important to Ted but not near as important as having decent clothes and shoes to go to school. Appearance is paramount in an adolescent's perception, and he no longer felt as if he stood out.

Believe me, all of this work was difficult and much tougher for Ted. Some of his family was not encouraging and angry with his success (as they viewed it as our changing Ted). This was difficult for Ted to face, accept, and cope.

Many of the families I have worked with welcome the success of their child but wonder if they can sustain such upon return home. A few like Ted's resent the changes. When Ted changed, they too had to acknowledge a change in their relationship and role... their behavior had to change as Ted's was not reverting to his old form.

Long story short... Ted graduated eighth grade, B honor roll if I remember correctly, but not without numerous struggles and issues. It was a difficult year of growth for Ted and at times he wanted to give up and force us to give up. Like the butterfly, changing and growing is not without a lot of pain.

Chapter 5
How do I talk with Johnny? Keys to effective communication.

"Happiness is a butterfly, which when pursued, is always just beyond your grasp, but which, if you will sit down quietly, may alight upon you." -Nathaniel Hawthorne

Two things we know about communication that are constant and universal:

1) We are always communicating. We cannot NOT communicate.

2) We may not be speaking, but a message is being sent and received.

Numerous studies have proven the above two statements and the work of Dr. Albert Merabian of U.C.L.A., as early as 1969, and as recently as 2006 emphasize that the message being sent, received, and interpreted is based more on our tone of voice and facial expression than actual verbal content.

Meaning received (especially by people in a crisis or under stress) is received through:

Facial Expression: 55%

Tone of Voice: 38%

Actual Words: 7%

This is particularly true with children and even more critical for children who have experienced trauma. Their safety and survival has depended on their ability to "read adults" and the warning signs.

So what does Johnny and other children like him "look out for?" He watches your body language, facial expression, where your hands are (as these are the weapons which he has had to defend against) and overall space issues, i.e. proximity, exits, safety routes for escape.

It is important that you be aware of these thoughts and issues going through Johnny's mind so you can adapt and adjust your behavior accordingly.

Along with the awareness of how we communicate with Johnny, as to his thoughts, feelings, and concerns, we need to learn how to become more effective communicators.

One of the key means to effective communication is the practice of "active listening," or "congruent listening." For our purposes, and the most common phrase used is "active listening."

What is this and how do you do it?

It involves your body, facial expression, eye contact, and minimal verbal responses to encourage Johnny to talk and begin to sort out his feelings, thoughts, and behaviors. To be effective, all of the above need to be "congruent."

Eye contact is essential, so you want to drop what it is you are doing, unless engaged in a mutual activity with Johnny, sit down at his level or lower and let him "see into" your eyes, which notifies him you are engaged.

"These lovely lamps, these Windows of the Soul."
-DuBartas

"And the eyes disclosed what the eyes alone could tell."
-Timothy Dwight

"In one soft look what language lies."
-Charles Didbin

Use your body and face, nods of the head, smiles, puzzled looks if indicated, leaning forward a little bit, without infringing on his personal space, SILENCE while he speaks and thinks, and very short verbal responses that encourages Johnny to tell you more, (even when you are dead sure you know what is going on). I have young people tell me quite often that they like a certain teacher or adult because that person listens to them even if the adults knows what is about to be said or where the conversation is going.

As to SILENCE being a form of communication, I am reminded of Mother Teresa's comment, *"Silence is the language God speaks. Everything else is a bad translation."*

Silence allows us to really hear and feel the message Johnny is trying to convey.

Kids are notorious for stopping mid-statement and saying things like, "I bet you have heard this before," or, "Am I bothering you?" My usual response is, "If it is important to you it is important to me, talk to me in the way you feel most comfortable."

These "minimal encouragements" can be "Uh huh," or "OK" or "I see," or "No kidding," or "Really," or "Tell me about that," or one of my favorites, "No crap!" This affords Johnny the opportunity to think a little more and talk on, without feeling like he is being rushed or as if you have judged him. Remember, young people in general have the feeling that "Nobody cares," and "Nobody listens," especially the adults involved in their lives.

The "minimal encouragements" also keep the conversation flowing and affords you the opportunity to learn more, not jump to conclusions, and think before offering your advice or comments.

As your discussion continues, you may want to ask "open ended" questions to get clarification and help Johnny think or rethink previous comments. Such questions often start with the words "How..." or "What..." such as "Johnny, how did you feel when _____?" or "What did you think when ____?"

Be cautious in using questions that start with "Why...," as such can be interpreted as "put downs," or criticism. As your relationship with Johnny develops and such discussions become easier, you may move pretty fast through the encouragement phase on to gathering information and helping him clarify events, feelings, and thoughts.

Please remember body language, tone of voice, and facial expressions are making the key contributions to your message and either encouraging or discouraging Johnny to respond.

As you begin using these brief verbal responses and comments you are moving into a more active "active listening" role.

During this phase of communication it is very important to focus on the "feeling" behind the verbal comment and be able to "reflect" this feeling. Neither Johnny nor any other child I have known truly cares if you understand their message... but each and every one wants their "feelings to be heard."

When you don't know what to do in such an encounter... REFLECT THE FEELING BEING EXPRESSED.

Reflecting feelings, or formulating the "reflective response" takes some practice and conditioning as it is may be a new way for many of us to speak with children as we have been conditioned to think of our feelings first and needs first, or to formulate an answer for a child without consideration of his feelings.

Looking at a couple of examples may help.

Johnny walks in from school, slams his books on the table and in a loud emotion laden voice yells, "I ain't going back to that stupid school, I hate that f---ing teacher!"

Our old conditioned response, which is of course very tempting, "Watch your language, young man!" or "Come on, Johnny, you don't really hate Mr. _____" or "I won't tolerate that attitude about school and teachers in my house."

The needed response, the reflective response in conjunction with eye contact, attention, and body language, to keep Johnny talking, engaged, and to begin de-escalation, would sound something like this, "Geez, Johnny, you really sound upset," or "Johnny, you sound angry."

DO NOT MINIMIZE HIS FEELINGS—such as... "Oh Johnny it's nothing, you'll feel better tomorrow." If you do Johnny hears this, "Your feelings are nothing, your feelings are stupid, your feelings are immature, your feelings are not important, etc. etc."

DO NOT MAXIMIZE HIS FEELINGS—such as... "Man you are right, Mr. _____is an "a –hole!"

Johnny will then hear confirmation and think, "Damn right I'll get that S.O.B. tomorrow." His feelings, thoughts, and subsequent behaviors will escalate, rather than de-escalate and become subject for discussion and reconsideration.

It is easy to fall into the trap of over support and enabling of Johnny. Many well intentioned "substitute parents" might have responded, "Look Johnny, I'm going with you to school and speak with the principal and get this set straight." At this point you do not know enough as to what took place to make such a commitment and it very well may not be needed. Johnny needs to learn from you how to advocate for himself and also how to ask for your help if and when needed.

The "reflective response" does not connote approval, consent, or acceptance.

I feel as if I need to reiterate the last sentence all the way to the end of the page as so many of us feel by listening we are sending the message of agreement. FALSE.

It simply reflects the feeling expressed and engages Johnny to talk out, talk about, and talk through whatever the situation or crisis might be. Forget the content and formulating a plan... that can come later after the feelings are "drained."

To do this well you may need to expand and enhance your emotional vocabulary, and in the process hopefully enhance and expand Johnny's. So many of the children I have worked with had a limited, and inappropriate, vocabulary. This inability to express themselves led to conflicts and escalation during emotional or crisis situations with parents, teachers, friends, police, etc. They often grope for a word, can't come up with it, and therefore fail to convey their real meaning. (The older I get the better I understand this futile attempt to grasp a needed work or name, only to come up short until given time to think!)

Johnny, like many children, know and rely on three basic emotional words to express his feelings... MAD, SAD, and GLAD, or the more dubious versions, Pissed, Down, and High.

Being limited in emotional vocabulary in effect traps Johnny in a snare that offers limited means of escape. When a young person expresses himself without thinking and inappropriately, few adults give them a chance to "take those words back" and such words tend to haunt Johnny and result in repercussions much more severe than when an adult slips up and says the same things.

I do not know why it is but we seem to give adults more opportunities to mess up and make amends than we do kids. Maybe it is our overwhelming need to, "teach that young man some manners," or the feeling that if we let him slide this one time, he will be encouraged to keep acting in this manner. If Johnny limits himself to feeling Mad, Sad, and Glad, he does not have as many responses and he sees himself as walking around with a cloud over his head, expecting and waiting for the rain (the emotion) to fall, except on those rare occasions when he is GLAD.

Johnny is Mad, therefore Johnny acts in a certain manner he has always acted when he is Mad. The same goes for when he is Sad. Johnny sees his feelings as "states of being," that cannot be altered, must be lived with, and acted upon in the old tried and true ways (even though those ways have led to more difficulties)... he does not see those feelings as something he can identify, modify and/or regulate.

As we listen and reflect his feelings, we can assist Johnny in obtaining a more diverse vocabulary that offers more ways of coping.

When Johnny gets MAD, he has thoughts about that feeling, engages in "self-talk," all in a "nano" second, then acts on this feeling/thought/ self-talk "cocktail", with his behavior usually being an ineffective, irrational, and/or unhealthy habitual response.

Let's say you get Johnny to understand that you can be irritated and frustrated, and that these feelings can be handled in a milder form than when feeling Mad. He has at least learned two new words to express an emotion and this affords him the opportunity to cope in a new and more effective manner. The positive for him in this effort is that his new manner of coping will most likely not cost him as much as the consequences will be less severe. Using terms that are de-escalating, maybe just a degree or two less severe, helps Johnny to think, gather his emotions and thoughts, and begin to see things a little more clearly.

Remember, Johnny is doing all of this with his "adolescent brain," not our, hopefully, "mature, adult brain."

When upset, Johnny often does not know what he is feeling or how to deal with the feeling. It is your obligation to help him better understand his own feelings and thoughts... without making a judgment.

REFLECTING A FEELING DOES NOT COMMUNICATE ACCEPTANCE OR AGREEMENT.

As you listen and reflect, you give him time to "drain" his emotions (venting) and slow down his thought process while you are modeling and teaching those exact same coping skills—you slow down, you don't overreact, you take time to think, then you act/respond.

Three questions that help Johnny develop this skill are...

1) What am I feeling?

2) What am I telling myself about this feeling?

3) What is my best response/reaction, based upon the answers to #1 and #2?

If you can get Johnny to go through these questions then whatever his response is for #3 you have to give it credibility as it should be less destructive or detrimental than his first reaction. Remember, we are only looking for a better response, not the perfect response.

If you feel his course of action is still too negative, then get back with him again, later, and walk through possible consequences and rewards of whatever behavior he proposed for #3. This teaches that reevaluation is also a good tactic in life.

As you discuss these various crises or problems with Johnny there will be times you think he is off on the wrong foot or very mistaken. First remember to listen as you will never get him started on a better path if you don't give him the opportunity to express himself.

Once you have a tentative grip on the feelings and Johnny has had ample time to sound off with your full attention you can move on to getting more information about what actually took place at school... this is the next step in the process, helping him clarify what took place.

During this step you may be surprised to hear from Johnny that this is the first time an adult has truly tried to listen to his version of events and how he was feeling. You might further be surprised to learn that although Johnny might have not handled this the way you would have, he was closer to the right path and may have a legitimate grievance with Mr._____.

Remember, a "talking Johnny" is an engaged Johnny and is therefore not an enraged Johnny and an "acting out" Johnny.

A talking Johnny is in effect searching for possible solutions, with your help. As you connect to his feelings, he will be more apt to give you credit as someone who might actually care and be of help.

This is the time to restate Johnny's ideas in your own words—a subtle way of "shaping" a new perspective for him—and check with him on whether you are close or not to his feelings and perceptions. You can use this time to encourage him to provide more information and then summarize what it is you think he told you. When you do the summary, just let him know what you are actually doing it (that sounds simple and it would not be necessary when talking with a friend or another adult).

"OK Johnny, let me try to summarize and see if I have the facts straight. You know sometimes having someone rephrase the story helps me to look at things in a different light." It is an introduction to another needed skill, to take a look back and start the process of self-critical thinking.

If he corrects your version, that is great, he is engaged and learning. Take that time to gain more information. You can also compare this episode to other such issues and ask if he has had similar situations and how were those handled by him and what was the outcome. Young people need our help making connections to current behavior to patterns of previous behavior as they tend to think in the moment and struggle to see the patterns and connections.

Doing so helps you to get Johnny to see whether he has had better success in the past or worse results. He can then be engaged to start looking at alternatives and strategies, sometimes the simple question, "Johnny, if you could go back, how might you handle this situation in a more positive manner for you? Don't worry about Mr. _____ right now, think what you might have done so the consequences to you were not so severe?" Get his ideas and strategies prior to introducing your own, as Johnny will not give yours consideration unless you have given his the respect deserved, or he will jump on yours just to stop the discussion, but will most likely not follow through. If he does follow through and the plan does not work, then it is, in his mind, "your crappy plan that failed."

Is this hard work, you betcha!! Modeling and teaching any skill is hard work, especially the all too rare skill of active listening. Every time I have such an encounter with a young person I get anxious and think, "Oh boy, Gary, I hope you are up to listening and keeping your big mouth shut. Geez, I hope I know the right thing to do when it is my opportunity to speak."

You may be like me and once we have a little success and have Johnny talking it is very easy to over step our boundaries and start dominating the discussion. This is very tempting to do to expedite the flow of the conversation to get where we need to go (and most likely will arrive there at the end of the process). After all, we got into these "substitute" roles to be HELPFUL. If you truly want to HELP, honor Johnny by honoring the process, as the process is your avenue to model and teach necessary skills and, most importantly, build the relationship. It is similar to the fish/fishing analogy; is a hungry man better off being given a fish to eat, or being taught how to fish for himself?

Obviously if the man was starving we would feed him first, then teach him how to provide for himself. There will be occasions where Johnny is "starving" and we will need to supply immediate help, but most of the time we need to slow down and get in the process of teaching him how to fish for himself.

I know this can be a problem for us "substitutes," as it was a major problem of mine when I first started in this work.

Even after a few years of working and hopefully improving, while working on my Master's degree in counseling I was admonished by one of my professors for "stepping on the lines" of my client. His criticism was that in my rush to help I did not give the client time to work through some of the feelings and thoughts. His analogy was in the field of acting. His point was I could be a great actor, know all of my lines, have great skills, and everything that needed to be known; BUT if I rushed my script lines and stepped on the lines of the other actors, I ruined the scene as it was not allowed to develop on its own. He also cautioned that doing so would inhibit the client, pushing him to either reply without due diligence or shut down. What was needed was for me to keep my "educated mouth shut," reflect the client's feelings, and let the scene play out. This is especially true with children as it takes them more time to get a grip on their feelings and thoughts.

When it came to "stepping on lines," I was not the only guilty party. One father I worked with was notorious in his family for not letting people complete their statements. It had cost him his marriage, according to his ex-wife, and was seriously jeopardizing his very limited relationship with his sixteen year old son, Jerome. At the time Jerome was placed in our facility, he and his father were barely speaking and both saw spending time together as a chore to be completed. Jerome did not know his father felt that way but suspected as much. His father had no idea "what's wrong with this boy," who did not want to go fishing with his dad or spend time together. No doubt these two people were very different individuals and Dad was a dominating person who wanted, and thought he had the male parental right, to have the first, middle, and last word in any conversation, ours included when we first met.

Jerome, had his issues too, but was pretty much a kind hearted kid and he warned me constantly that I had never dealt with a guy quite lack his dad. It was ironic but Jerome's mother could see both sides of her ex-husband and felt he wanted to be a good father but did not know how.

During our few talks we had prior to meeting with Jerome we discussed these concerns and perceptions. My major assistance to this family was to get Dad to be silent long enough to let Jerome finish his statements. Dad's consent was partially voluntary and also due to my decision not to work with them as a family if he could not at least try one simple session utilizing a ploy with me, unknown to Jerome. The ploy was that when Jerome spoke, Dad was to remain silent. If he started to interrupt, I would raise my hand with the palm up facing him, my sign to him to "shut up and listen" until Jerome stopped speaking. Dad then had my OK to say whatever he wanted, I did not care if he even attempted "active listening" skills, I just wanted his silence.

"Silence is one of the great arts of conversation."
-Hannah More

When I told Jerome that he, dad and I were going to sit down and talk about a few things, he was highly skeptical and let me know I would see his "real dad." Jerome had informed me they had been in "counseling" before and dad did not believe in it nor listen to anyone, including the counselor. I told Jerome I was just asking both to come and his part was to talk honestly with his dad, something that caused him considerable anxiety.

Jerome did his part, and as expected, Dad attempted to interrupt, but did stop when I put my hand up. Jerome was encouraged by this development and said more in the first get together than I ever expected, and to his credit, Dad took it without comment until it was his "turn."

Dad was a competitive spirit, totally opposite of Jerome (I believe he was non-competitive due to his father being super competitive and probably from losing in many, many situations to his dad). If they fished, Dad had to catch the most fish and let everyone know it. Dad admitted to being competitive and driven to succeed. I tapped into this competitive spirit by making a bet with Dad as to how many times he would interrupt his son during our talks. It was an easy bet such as, "I'm willing to bet you can do this if you try, but I'm also willing to bet you butt in at least X times." Dad took the challenge, and we would compare notes following to see how many times he did interrupt. Dad won every time and beat my anticipated number, which is what I was hoping.

Overall improvement took time and more practice, but once his silence worked, Dad was more willing to try other things like reflecting his son's feelings... wow, what an adventure for Dad, Jerome, and me.

Again I utilized the wager ploy and again Dad beat my bet.

I am not sure at any time he actually "bought in" completely with what we were doing, but the dividends did come as their relationship improved and Jerome was much more amenable to spending more time with his father. Dad was able to acknowledge the progress made and felt his relationship with his son, although not what he always dreamed, it was better. Jerome's comments reflected the same as to his dad. One of the last weekends Jerome was in placement, he and his dad had a visit where they did go fishing without competition and both, independently and somewhat grudgingly, admitted to having a good time. Jerome never felt he would be like his dad, nor did he want to be, but he did want a relationship with him.

Not all of the families end with this kind of success. Strengths they had, and were recognized, were both wanted an improved relationship and were willing to let someone help. Dad took a little more responsibility as the adult to try new strategies and skills.

It was interesting to me that the first step was not some outpouring of understanding, warmth, regret, and acceptance... it was Dad being SILENT and letting his son hear his own voice as well as Dad hearing it, too.

We need to honor the silences and gaps in conversation as this allows Johnny time to think and contemplate what was just said. I used the word contemplate as that denotes deeper thinking about something, another slight change on the word think. We are always thinking, but how often do we contemplate. Model and teach that word, and the skill that goes with it, usually taking a little time before reacting. Guard against cutting in on his lines with your own words you think he may be searching for… let him do the search and exploration. Watch jumping to conclusions, such exercise does not burn calories but may char a relationship!

When we interrupt, we stop effective communication and children are prone to go along with the adult thoughts or comments, never revealing their true feelings. Far too often when a young person tells me, "My parents don't understand," he really means, "My parents don't listen," which can be carried to this end, "My parents don't let me finish my point." If charged with the above during my days as a parent, I am sure I could have been convicted too many times. I am also afraid I do the same, at times, in my "substitute" role.

In my work with children and my time as a parent I do know ONE THING FOR SURE… I have never regretted keeping my mouth shut and biting my tongue to do so… I regret far too many times opening my mouth too soon and too often.

Abraham Lincoln said it best:

"It is better for me to stand here silent and appear stupid, rather than open my mouth and remove all doubt."

At the end of this chapter I will have a partial list of feelings for your perusal and use. Most young people I have known and worked with are deficient in vocabulary to express how and what they are feeling and thinking.

To get kids to "talk" we need to allow them to use their own words.

I want the young person when I first meet him to feel free to talk with me any way he so desires… IF the conversation is in private. I do not care as to his choice of words at this stage… it can be proper English, slang, crude, profane; none of this matters as long as he is talking. I do make a differentiation to private and public conversation. The example I use is, "Look, we will need to be able to talk with one another. I don't care if it's just the two of us what you say or how you say it, including profanity and profanity directed at me. Now if I'm walking through the dining room I do not want you to holler, "Hey you stupid S.O.B., I need to see you. As to calling me a stupid S.O.B. in private—no problem—although I prefer Gary." I also let him know that in the course of living at our facility and working with staff he will learn new and more effective and appropriate ways of expressing his feelings, wants, needs, joys and sorrows, and that we will treat him with respect and not be verbally abusive, regardless of the situation.

There are also some things NOT TO DO, when communicating with children unless you want to lose your audience. The following are guaranteed to STOP communication with a child.

SARCASM: Kids don't "get" adult sarcasm, even when it is meant and delivered as humor. They see it as personal and let the words define the meaning.

Stay away from it until you have a very good relationship and then be sure to explain it upon use.

DISBELIEF: Listen carefully before you disregard what a child is telling you. You would be sickened at the number of children who have divulged deep hurtful things to me, only to inform me they had done so before and were not believed. Some were not believed by parents, teachers, social workers, clergy, police, family members, and friends. It takes courage to divulge hurtful secrets. Please don't reply, "Oh come on, you know that isn't true," or "I heard you were quite a liar," or "Why should I believe you," and I could go on and on.

I had one experience that I will never forget (and quite honestly I have not forgiven).

A family case manager was meeting with a young man, Dennis, and me in my office. He had recently divulged important family matters involving his mother beating him with a wooden chair. During our discussion I asked Dennis if he had reported this to anyone, and he had, in fact more than one person, but nothing was done. Due to his disclosure I asked his case manager to meet with us, only to find out that she, too, had been told and failed to follow up. I was not aware of this until our discussion started, Dennis became very upset, sobbing and kept saying over and over, "But I told you." This particular case manager refused to listen and kept interrupting and protesting until I stepped in and forcefully told her to, "Be quiet, and listen to Dennis. You are still refusing to hear him!"

How frustrating this must have been to Dennis to have the person who he was supposed to trust not even afford him the common courtesy of listening. I am sorry to say that case manager never did anything else, but Dennis felt better finally getting his attention and telling his story.

I would love to say to you that this was an isolated case, but that would be false. One of the most significant things we can do for our kids in our care are allow them to tell their story and then see to it that such revelations are properly handled. You will at times find out you are the first to have been told, respond, and report. This was a "watershed" moment for Dennis just to get it out, even if one of the listeners tried to turn a blind eye and deaf ear to the screams of this particular butterfly.

Maya Angelou once wrote, *"There is no greater agony than bearing an untold story inside you."*

I will agree with that but would beg to differ to a degree, the greatest agony would be telling the story and NO ONE LISTENS... NO ONE RESPONDS!

SHAMING: Anyone who has been shamed or embarrassed knows how this stings and scars. It stings because of the immediate pain, it scars as it stays with children. One young man, Donny, age ten, had a bedwetting problem. I was working with him and his mother to get him back home out of foster care. His mother asked that I talk with his dad who kept calling Donny "pee baby" every day following an accident. Unfortunately, Donny's dad did not want to talk with any counselor about anything and this continued and was a factor in delaying his return home. Donny was in a very good foster home and making great strides in all areas, including the enuresis, but he did not go home until his parents separated (more due to his father's drinking than choice of humiliating words).

MINIMIZING: Another great put down to children. "Oh come on, it couldn't be that bad," or "Give it time, you'll get over it." We tend to minimize when we view the world of a child through our adult eyes and speak that way. Will kids get over some things with time, sure they will, just like we did and do, but to them if they are telling you it hurts or they are in great joy, don't degrade their pain and PLEASE do not rain on their parade, most enjoy so few.

LABELING: Children are people first and foremost, not a can of soup which has a label listing ingredients, calories, and what not. A child may have been diagnosed as ADHD, but we should never talk with the child using that label, such as, "Well you know you are ADHD so no Kool Aid for you tonight." This seems so obvious of a caveat, but it happens all of the time. "Hey these are my three kids and this is Johnny our foster son." You would not look at that example as labeling, but look at it through Johnny's eyes and imagine how he felt when he heard the distinction.

DISTRACTING: Now this can help de-escalate a child from time to time, but when Johnny is talking, don't change the subject or focus. If you are lucky and build a strong relationship, you are going to hear things from him that you would love to change the subject or focus from as these things cause you discomfort. When you distract or shift focus, Johnny's thought will be, "They don't want to hear the stuff I really need their help with," or even worse, "They must have thought I was weird cause they sure as heck did not want to talk about it."

ARGUING: Stay away from getting into an argument and power struggle with a child, you will never win either. Think, "Am I getting into a duel-logue rather than a dialogue?"

BLAMING: The kids I know have enough shame and blame to last two life times. Please don't add yours. I had a foster parent who was a master at blaming her foster daughter in a subtle manner. "Well I hope you enjoyed that movie. It costs me $16 and I did not like it, so I don't want to hear I don't love you!" That is almost a direct quote. You can probably guess how this relationship ended as the child heard, "Poor me, I suffer and give to this kid who does not appreciate me. What is wrong with this child?"

PREACHING: I saw a statement on a church outdoor sign that sums this one up, it said, "Practice what you Preach! Never mind, forget the Preaching, just Practice!" Your message is received better by walking the walk rather than talking, talking, and more talking the talk.

INTERRUPTING: See the previous pages and "stepping on lines."

NAGGING: If you have to say it more than three times in a ten minute time period, you are nagging and the young person hears, "Blah, blah, blah, bitch and moan, moan and bitch." Nagging tends to enrage or at best get the child to tune out; it does not engage and encourage discourse.

Being an effective communicator and an active listener takes practice and patience. If you are sincerely attentive, most children will give you a break, even if you slip into one of the above every once in a while. Kids are forgiving to those who are genuine and practice forgiveness. If you MESS UP, FESS UP, make amends, and keep moving forward; another skill we can model.

"Flatter me, and I may not believe you. Criticize me and I may not like you. Ignore me and I may not forgive you. Encourage me and I may not forget you."
-William Arthur

FEELING WORDS:

Abandoned Accepting Accused Adamant Adequate Admired Adventurous Affected Affectionate Afraid Aggravated Agitated Alarmed Alienated Amazed Ambivalent Amiable Amused Angry Anxious Apathetic Appalled Astonished Awed Awkward Awesome

Bad Baffled Battered Beaten Beautiful Befuddled Betrayed Bitter Brave

Calm Capable Carefree Careless Caring Caught Challenged Comfortable Committed Compassionate Competent Concerned Confident Confused Conscientious Considerate Crazy Crippled Critical Curious

Daring Dead Debilitated Defensive Defiant Delirious Depressed Desperate Destructive Disappointed Discontented Discourage Disgusted Distant Distraught Disturbed Divided Doubtful Dubious Dumb Dutiful

Eager Effective Embarrassed Emotional Empty Empathetic Encouraged Energetic

Enraged Exasperated Excited Exhausted

Fascinated Fearful Flexible Floundering Flustered Frightened Frustrated

Gloomy Good Great Grief Guilty Gullible

Handicapped Happy Harassed Harried Hateful Helpless Hopeful Horrible

Horrified Hostile

Ignorant Immature Inadequate Incompetent Indignant Ineffective Infuriated

Interested Intimidated Involved Isolated

Lost Melancholy Mixed emotions Motivated Mystified Neutral Nervous

Odd Outraged Overburdened Overwhelmed Overworked

Pained Pensive Perplexed Perturbed Pity Positive Powerful Powerless Prepared

Protective Provoked Puzzled

Rage Rational Regretful Relaxed Religious Remorseful Resentful Resistive Right

Sad Scared Self-confident Sensitive Shocked Shunned Shy Sick Startled Superior

Suspicious

Tense Terrible Terrified Timid Tired Tolerant Traumatized Turned on Turned off

Uncaring Uncomfortable Understanding Uneasy Unfriendly Unhappy Unique

Unprepared Unsettled Unsure Unwanted Uptight Useless

Vehement Violent Vulnerable

Weak Willing Wishing Worthless Worthy

As stated before, children who have experienced trauma often have great difficulty in expressing and processing verbal statements. The above terms can help those children increase their vocabulary, define and express their feelings, and "talk" about their problems with a caring, supportive, understanding adult—important steps in coping, exercising improved self-control, and being understood.

Chapter 6
What do I do when Sarah gets upset or angry?

"We delight in the beauty of the butterfly, but rarely admit the changes it has gone through to achieve that beauty."
-Maya Angelou

A word to the reader: as noted in the Introduction, I am, and recommend that you be, "eclectic" in your reading, methods, and techniques. The following information is what I have found to be effective and can transfer to your particular situation.

I do not propose to have all of the answers and I am hopeful that this presentation will pique your interest and desire to learn more.

I am in debt to those authorities and experts cited and noted throughout this book, but especially so in this chapter.

As adults in the "substitute" role, the children we are engaged with often have major emotional issues and great difficulty regulating their reactions, be it anger, rage, sadness, a feeling of being lost and disconnected, and major grief.

1) They have good reason to be upset, angry, depressed, anxious, and grieving.

2) Many have experienced trauma in their lives, abuse (sexual and physical), severe neglect, loss of a loved one, abandonment, and neglect of basic needs, just to name a few.

3) They do not know how to effectively, rationally, and in a healthy safe manner handle such emotions and deal with the trauma they have experienced. Their coping skills are usually significantly deficient.

Hopefully not every child you come into contact with in your efforts will be severely traumatized, but one trauma can be of huge significance and have tremendous impact in their lives.

It is my belief that any child who has experienced separation from his family has had a "traumatic" experience.

Based on research, including brain imaging, there are some things we know about children who have had trauma experiences, unfortunately there is not a lot of "good news" to report. However, I am including this information so you have an informed idea of the behaviors and factors impacting these young people's lives.

Trauma is not "fixed" and almost always leaves scars, some physical as well as psychological, developmental, social, and emotional. Trauma can impact how the brain functions and we are seeing more evidence of trauma induced neurological damage.

The longer the duration of the trauma, such as early child sexual abuse, continues, the more severe the damage.

If the abuse is severe in nature the damage is more severe.

If the abuser is close to the child (and most perpetrators are well known to their victims, unfortunately often members of the child's family), the more severe the damage.

Traumatized children can show different symptoms but some that are common are:

Intensity of Feelings

Impulsiveness

Difficulty processing verbal messages

Focus is on what is necessary to survive

Anger is reactive and easily triggered

Memory loss

If treated, often these victims are misdiagnosed as:

Attention Deficit/Hyperactive ADHD and Oppositional Defiant Disorder ODD

In severe cases, the child might exhibit behavior that appears unattached, distant, "zoned out," and/or submissive, as if he has "surrendered" to his life experiences. The list above is not inclusive and I am in no means an expert in the field, although I have worked with hundreds of trauma victims.

What we do know is that a critical key, one of the top two, to a child "adapting" to and learning coping skills is a healthy and supportive relationship with an adult who has an understanding of the trauma and a commitment to the child. The other key factor is the native intellect of the child.

We also know that this is a "real" and costly societal problem.

Statistics compiled by the U.S. Department of Health and Human Services in 2009 reveal how widespread this issue is and the long term effects of such on people's lives.

In the U.S. deaths since 1998 have steadily increased from 3.13 to 5+ per 100,000 as of 2009. An official report of child abuse is logged every 10 seconds.

Of the deaths, over 1,700 annually, 80% of the victims are under age four years.

It is estimated that 50% to 60% of child fatalities reported are due to abuse but not recorded as such.

90% of juvenile sexual victims knew their perpetrator.

30% of victims will victimize their own or other children.

80% of 21 year olds receiving services for a psychological disorder report being a trauma victim as a child.

Victims of abuse are 59% more likely to have a juvenile delinquent record, are 28% more likely to have an adult arrest record, and are 30% more likely to commit a violent crime.

Parents who are substance abusers are three times more likely to mistreat their children.

67% of people in substance abuse treatment report a childhood history of trauma. Young women who are abused are 25% more likely to become pregnant while a teen.

14% of men in prison report childhood trauma and 36% of women report the same.

In 2009, 3.3 million reports were received involving six million children under age 18 years. The last report indicated that 500,000 children are seriously harmed.

Although the estimated cost of such childhood trauma for 2008 was 124 billion dollars, the U.S. is the worst industrialized country in this category.

These are not my statistics or measurements. I provide them so you have a glimpse of how pervasive and damaging such trauma can be to our children.

It is important to remember the above information and not to OVEREACT or MINIMIZE the impact on our kids. It is also important to remember not to OVEREACT or MINIMIZE the emotions and behaviors Sarah is likely to exhibit.

Anger is an emotion Sarah is familiar with and "comfortable" with, i.e. she knows how to be angry and its benefits or purposes. Sarah also knows it can be a great field leveler, i.e. if Sarah can get us angry; she has more experience dealing and handling "angry adults" than rationale adults. Therefore it levels the playing field so we are all on the same emotional level. As mentioned before, when we are at our angriest, we are at our "stupidest." Intense anger drops our intellectual functioning down to a level that Sarah can more readily match wits with and manage.

Anger or acting emotionally upset may also be a means of keeping distance from an adult, including you. Sarah may have learned, if I get angry adults leave me alone; if I act emotional, people give me space or sometimes meet my demands, "emotional blackmail."

And then again, Sarah may have darn good reason to be upset and/or angry. It could be her way of opening up her world of pain and giving you a glimpse, hoping you will recognize, acknowledge, and help her.

When a child is emotionally distraught, and/or is faced with a conflict, especially one that has a degree of personal risk or harm, there are basically four ways the child can choose to respond

1) Fight

2) Flight

3) Submit

4) Posture

FIGHT

To fight back is often the first choice she relies on as it is how she has handled many of the conflicts in her life and protected herself from harm. This is the "reactive" anger very common to child trauma victims.

FLIGHT

To flee or take flight is also a means of handling conflict and we see this in a sad or depressed child who will try to "flee" from her internal conflicts. Fleeing or "running away" can be the recourse of the youngster who is confused and or conflicted about her new situation, home, parents, tasks, expectations, school, etc. Any kind of change or transitional period tends to induce more stress on the child. There are some things the child cannot fight or resist, so to flee is a natural response. At times their means of fleeing are unhealthy choices—cutting behaviors, running away, using drugs or alcohol, etc.

SUBMIT

To submit is maybe the most worrisome response I have seen in children. To give in and give up, to accept the hand life has dealt her can be tragic. A child who seems listless and displays little emotion, worries me as I know the emotions are inside, bottled up, and when they are eventually "let loose" much harm can often be the result. The "letting loose" might be external, easier for us to see and deal with, or internal, much more difficult to understand and provide assistance.

POSTURE

To posture is often the response utilized by a child who is new to a situation and faced with a conflict she does not know how to handle. To act in a manner that tends to keep people at arms-length, one of bravado or at times aloofness, as if to say, "Don't you dare try to get close to me." This child has probably had to posture a lot in her short life due to so many conflicts and changes she has faced. When you think of posturing, think of military conflicts in history, where armies lined up and tried to intimidate their foes without actually engaging in combat, screaming, shooting over their heads, banging shields, etc. (There is more information coming out on posturing and one of the best books I have read involving this behavior in the military is "*On Killing*" by Lt. Col. Dave Grossman.)

There is nothing inherently wrong with any of these responses to conflict. Let's face it, at times we all use parts of all four to handle the conflict in our adult lives.

It is how we modify this response that usually makes us more effective than Sarah. So as "substitute parents," how do we instill or advance Sarah's skills in those responses?

The following questions might sound peculiar upon first reading, and they even sound odder when we start framing them in our own minds.

How might we help her become a better fighter, without increasing her anger and aggression? Usually we start with tempering the reactive aggression to one of reactive assertiveness, standing up for herself without losing control or harming herself or others.

How might we help Sarah become a better "runner," when it is the best strategy to flee? Think along the lines of ignoring, choosing to disengage, walking away from a confrontation, taking "time and space" for herself… not actually turning tail and eloping per se. It is a controlled strategy of retreat until you have time to rethink your options and develop a better and more effective coping strategy.

How might we improve her ability to submit without surrender, giving up, giving in, or putting herself at risk of harm? Again this would involve a strategic retreat from the conflict and seeking assistance from you, hopefully, to develop a better response. Sometimes that response can simply be your presence so no harm is done to her or by her to herself. Your "being there" affords her a partner in her dilemma if nothing else. Professional boxers rely upon their manager and coaches to help them, to be in their corner, making it more difficult to give up and holler, "No mas!"

What we want to do for Sarah is to give her a means of handling and dealing with these conflicts, external and internal, that cause her the least harm and afford the most growth. These coping skills need to be ones she can learn to utilize when you are not present and can be generalized from the specific.

Some questions to ask yourself prior to engaging Sarah are:

Of course the… BIG FOUR:

What am I feeling?

You have to have a grip on yourself before you can be of any assistance to Sarah.

What is Sarah feeling?

What is it Sarah needs?

What is my best response?

Along with these ask yourself, "What purpose does this behavior serve?"

Is this behavior normal or typical for Sarah?

Can this behavior be ignored or do I need to act? Sometimes attention seeking behavior can be ignored and we need to plan to do so, but that is rare and kids like Sarah have been ignored too often.

Is this behavior normal and expected for a child of Sarah's age or development?

Is this behavior a manifestation of a family response, belief, or norm?

The answers to this quick inventory may help you formulate a more effective helpful response.

Our goal is not to quash the anger or emotion being displayed.

Our goal should be to intervene with a response(s) to de-escalate Sarah and help her learn how to effectively manage the anger or emotion.

We want to intervene in a helpful supportive manner with Sarah so that she comes to realize her emotions are her choices. In a fashion she chooses to be angry, sad, happy, frustrated although she might not be as aware of this process as you and I are. No doubt her life experiences, especially the trauma, affects those choices, but they are still hers. We can help her develop and improve coping skills that will assist her in self-management, but no one's emotions can be micro managed from the outside, it is an internal process.

Some of the young people we engage are very capable of exerting this self-control in parts of their lives and need minimum assistance from us.

However, for kids feeling out of control it is important to emphasize that they can at least improve their self-control. They need to hear this message and get our support in their efforts in this endeavor, as after all it is their lives.

I have found a number of these young people look at adults, especially counselors, psychiatrists, teachers, and doctors as if we are magicians with special tricks or potions that we use to be successful in life. We need to remind them that we are not magicians; we have no super powers, pills, potions, or tricks. However, we can and do have some knowledge, experience, and methods that are fairly successful and we can help them obtain coping skills and learn new more effective, rational, and healthy ways of living.

The two major emotions I see exhibited by children are anger and sadness/depression. The following will primarily address those two emotions.

Let's start with an angry Sarah, not explosive yet, but escalating. How can we help her deescalate so we can address the entire issue?

The caveat here is that each child is different and Sarah's age, developmental history, reason for being in your care, length of stay, and your relationship with her all play a part in how you choose to intervene. Before intervening, think about what works well for you and her within the context of your relationship.

PHYSICAL PRESENCE

There are occasions when your mere presence can be a de escalator, i.e. proximity. Are you present, how close are you to the child, physically, and are you paying attention. Simply being there can have an immediate impact on Sarah's emotions, both positive and negative. That is why it is important to know what works with and for Sarah. In my experience, my presence and position within the facility has usually served as a de-escalator and I can intervene in a manner that is productive for the young person and lead to a better subsequent discussion.

CUES

If present you may intervene with simple cues, gentle positive reminders of behavior needed as opposed to the behavior displayed. To calmly remind Sarah to "calm down," "chill," "cool off," "breathe," may be all she needs on that occasion to gather herself and begin to deescalate. As you get to know Sarah and the language she uses, you will learn cues or prompts that she can relate to and will grab her attention. If you get the desired response you can then discuss with her how to build those cues into her own calming "self-talk."

What many children fail to understand is how anger and emotions work. It is important that we provide an understanding for them of their anger and stress so they can initiate their own calming skills... hopefully more appropriate than those presently used.

TRIGGERS AND BUTTONS

Anger usually starts with a perceived or present "trigger" or "button," pulled or pushed that starts the process. These "triggers" can be external (something happened in Sarah's immediate environment to impact her) or internal (a thought, memory, reminder, or feeling that impacts her). Getting Sarah to recognize her external and internal "triggers" is important to finding solutions and means of handling her anger.

Often early warning signs of a "trigger" existing involve physiological reactions, a feeling in the "gut," sweating, moist palms, increased heart rate, clenching of fists, teeth, etc. Helping her recognize these physical indicators is a good first step in her regulating her emotions and reactions.

Once the "trigger" is pulled Sarah has a feeling, then quickly tells herself something about that feeling, "self-talk," that then causes her to behave, which in turn leads to a consequence or reward. With anger, the self-talk is often negative, leading to a misbehavior that leads to a consequence which leads to more feelings and thoughts leading to more behavior, additional consequences, on and on and on... a cyclic escalation.

That is the typical way anger and strong emotions work in children and in reality all of us.

Managing the self-talk is essential. We can assist with cues and prompts that can mitigate the effect. When Sarah learns more about her "triggers" and the cyclic process she can utilize her own positive self-talk which can impact the results.

SHAPING

It is important to remember that like all skills, few of us become adept in one trial, with the same being true for young people. What we need to look for is improvement and the process is best described as "shaping." What we want is a better, more rational response each time the "trigger" is pulled. A demonstration of a new behavior and skill better than the old one requires you to provide positive reinforcement.

For example, Sarah becomes angry at school and throws a chair in class. As you discuss this with her and come up with more appropriate alternatives that she owns and will use, she needs your positive endorsement of the improvement, although it might not be exactly what you wanted or hoped. So the next day she returns to school, a positive in and of itself, becomes upset again, but this time she storms out of the class, using profanity towards the teacher. Give her credit first for not throwing the chair as she chose to take leave of the immediate environment, and although cursing, this is a considerable improvement over throwing objects that can physically hurt others.

Refrain from exaggeration and "blowing off" a child's feelings. To reduce the level of the emotion you want to "turn it down" a level or two.

For example, Sarah claims, "I hate him I'm going to kill that f'n' teacher!"

Your response, "Wow, you really sound upset, sounds to me like you want to tell him off?"

If the feeling is one of being minimalized, then the task is to "turn it up" a level or two.

For example, Sarah exclaims, "Oh I don't care he didn't call me, it's not that important." Your response, "Sarah, you sound a little disappointed, maybe it matters more than you are telling yourself?"

ACTIVE LISTENING

Anytime we are dealing with a child who is emotionally charged such as Sarah, it is absolutely vital to actively listen for the feelings of the message. Again don't overreact or get caught up in the actual content. The message is not near as important as the feeling within the message. Utilize the active listening skills we have mentioned throughout this book. Refer to Chapter 5: Keys to Effective Communication.

Tune in to the child.

Remain calm.

Identify the feeling by listening for it, and reflect such back.

Use open ended questions to gain information.

Focus on possible internal dynamics.

Don't judge or throw up roadblocks to communication.

Ignore insults.

Engage, engage, engage. If Sarah is talking she is not acting out.

As with all of us, when Sarah's anger increases, her reasoning skills go out the window and her intellect decreases commensurate with the level of emotion, thus increasing the likelihood of more radical behavior.

Retaliation might be tempting, especially after you have been called every name in the book plus some you never heard before, or maybe in a language you don't know. Resist the temptation.

"Well you know what happens when you wrestle with pigs; you get all dirty and the pigs love it!"
-Anonymous

Remember Sarah is upset and not engaged in using her intellect. If you allow yourself to get on her emotional level it becomes extremely difficult to climb back up and assume a helping position. Children like Sarah, especially when irate, have a knack of getting us caught up in the whole mess and engaging our anger. If you retaliate or engage in a "she said so I said" diatribe, Sarah will win the engagement just about every time. Her skills at this level are better than most adults. The sad truth is you both lose in the short and long term. You have lost an opportunity to teach and help, she has lost an opportunity to learn and benefit. The relationship has also suffered a serious setback.

DIALOGUE OR "DUEL-LOGUE"

Active listening affords you and Sarah time to think and calm down. You are beginning to promote a dialogue rather than a "duel-logue," i.e. a verbal sparring match that erodes the relationship and is counterproductive to your role.

Experiencing anger and angry thoughts is to be expected in your role as a substitute parent. Don't try to deny your true feelings, but learn how to get past them and do what you "know" is right, not what you "feel" is right. Manage your emotions to help Sarah learn how to manage hers.

I once worked with a group of siblings and had a decent relationship with two of the three as they matriculated through our program. The last of the group was Kyle when he was twelve years old. I thought my success with his other siblings would transfer to Kyle... boy was I wrong (I assumed, I made an ass of Kyle and me). Kyle was different than his older sister and brother, much more emotional and fragile, having experienced more trauma than his siblings, including a broken leg when hit by an automobile.

We eventually had to remove him from our program, due to his violence towards others, and placed him in a short term psychiatric facility. The actual moving experience was a "moving" experience. A colleague, who happened to be an older ex-Army sergeant, and I, along with a driver made the actual move in one of our station wagons. Kyle took offense to the move and we were involved in a physical struggle within the confines of the back seat of the car. I remember vividly Kyle's anger and he demonstrated such by repeatedly spitting in my face... the confines prevented me from turning my head. My colleague, Sam, who was on the other side, also received the same treatment and he could tell I was reaching my limit.

I was very tempted to inflict some sort of retaliation, holding him tighter, applying pressure to his sore leg, squeezing him, whatever, when Sam looked me in the eye, with spit running down his cheek, and simply smiled while slightly shaking his head signaling a silent, "No, don't do it, Gary." Sam had done three tours in Vietnam and had experienced some real hostility in his time. The thought ran through my mind, "If this old guy can take this crap, I can too." That smile saved me from getting into a retaliatory reaction and reminded me, "Your anger does not give you the right to lose your mind and do something stupid." Sam and I got through it, as did Kyle, and both Kyle and I owe Sam for keeping us both safe.

Since that day I have experienced a couple of more "spitters," and it never fails to bring back the visual reminder of Sam and his smile, and remind me of my obligations. If I fail to act in a therapeutic and helpful manner, regardless of the behavior exhibited by the child, then I as the adult have erred. If I act in a punitive and/or abusive manner I can do irreparable harm to the child... possibly physically, and for sure emotionally. Our relationship will have major problems getting back to one that is productive, and what respect the child had for me is lost.

I am responsible for setting the parameters of what is acceptable behavior in an encounter with an angry escalated child.

It has been my experience that the two major de-escalators of agitated angry children are...

TIME AND SPACE

Simply allowing Sarah time to think and sort out her feelings can have a huge impact on her immediate and future behavior. Time does heal or allow for healing in a lot of grievances. We have to allow the child the time to work through some of her feelings and thoughts about those feelings... IF, of course, the situation is not dangerous.

Given time, Sarah is more apt to listen and respond to our requests. Time affords her the opportunity to think through possible options or alternatives that are more appropriate. Simply stopping your interaction for a few minutes also allows you time to regroup, and removes her "duel-logue" partner... YOU.

Space is also very important for many of the same reasons as time. It decreases pressure on Sarah and you to perform or come up with a hasty response that complicates the situation. Remember to be very aware of personal space when a child is becoming angry or upset... a good rule of thumb is to double your normal personal space length. Also leave open an exit way for the child to increase her own space and time from you. If Sarah chooses to exit the area, allow it. That is a good skill she is utilizing, although her motives might be suspect, who cares? If you can get her to use her own time and space skills, you are providing her skills she can utilize all of her life.

I have had many a child walk away from me during an encounter. It is hard not to respond and insist they turn back and reengage. However, if I do, I am only asking for what I get, not re-engagement, but re-enragement. Later when we re-engage, I can address how to create time and space from me in a manner I do not misunderstand. I always start my re-engagement with a compliment to the youngster for seeing the need to disengage and ·get some time and space. Most of the time they do not recognize the skill, until I point it out as a skill, and provide a minor adjustment or two so the child can utilize it without incurring the wrath of an unskilled adult.

I have also turned the table before on a child, letting her know I needed some time and space to think and reconsider options. If you take the "time away" you are responsible for setting up the "time" to get back together. If you request a child to take "time away" it usually helps if you emphasize the mutuality, i.e. "Hey Sarah, we both need some 'time away' from this issue and each other, lets separate and try to get back together _____." Sarah might need more time and space when you try to reconvene, no big deal, grant it, but again let her set the new time to reconvene. It does not have to be minutes or hours, it might be later after dinner, when you take the dog for a walk, play basketball, go for a drive, run an errand, or some other activity you can do privately with her.

Always leave the door open for Sarah to reconvene earlier than you previously set. She may resolve the issue or decide it is no big deal.

Time, space, and "time away" allow for the stress and immediacy of the emotion to dissipate, the intensity "drain" or at least de-escalate.

"Time away" should not be confused with a "time out". "Time out" is a temporary cessation of the interaction, much like a time out called by a coach during a basketball game. It allows for a brief time to "cool off," refocus, and reconsider what needs to be done, with a return to the action imminent.

Be careful to avoid coming across as arbitrary. If you tell Sarah she needs a "time out" for X amount of minutes, you are very likely to be perceived as sentencing her to "do time." What you want is a brief cessation of the encounter that affords her time, the length depending on her assessment, to calm down and think.

Most children, when given a "time out" will focus on the time period, not the issue needing the focus. Such "time outs" can be escalators rather than a de-escalator as the child will sit, brood, and count the time left on his sentence, often becoming angrier with the focus of the anger being you, his "jailer." Sarah is most likely to keep bothering you as to when her "time" is up.

Put the burden on the child. If Sarah is asked to "time herself out" until she can discuss the issue without escalating, establish the ground rule that when she feels in control of herself you will be ready for her to return and, if necessary, talk. This might take her two minutes or ten; it does not matter as long as it is self-imposed. When she returns you are obligated to give the time and attention needed, and be sure, upon conclusion, to thank her for making the choice to cool off and work things out.

"Time away" or "Time out" should not be utilized in a manner whereas Sarah perceives it as going to jail.

You want her to perceive this intervention as time well spent gathering herself, refocusing, cooling off, for her return to be more productive and get on with her life.

As repeated throughout this book, building a relationship and getting to know the child is essential in helping. It is also essential when dealing with an angry or emotionally upset Sarah.

If you have had the time to establish a relationship, you have a better understanding of what is going on with her and what you might do to intervene.

If you have not had much time to build a relationship, believe me, going through such a crisis can be the first major step as Sarah will never be as susceptible to your influence as she is when she is in crisis. She will also be more apt to learn.

Some adults want to avoid or cover up a child being angry as the adult is uncomfortable dealing with anger or emotionality. If you do this you deny the child an excellent opportunity to grow.

Think back on your own life... when did you learn what you really needed to know? I am willing to guess most things we learn came out of the necessity to learn. We were in a situation or crisis where learning or adapting was extremely critical and important.

My father was a very reasonable man who would never have harmed my sister or me. He taught me to swim after I had "washed out" of swimming lessons at the local YMCA. He taught me in the Ohio River, first by having me practice everything essential next to him. I did OK with this, but when he put me in the river with him in the boat, his lessons came to life and I swam like my life depended on it (it did not, he was right there, but not in the water). When swimming became critical, I practiced what he had taught me, I was susceptible to learning as well as remembering and doing.

As you build a relationship with a child you have a better feel for what is not right, when she is upset, frustrated, really angry, etc. You get to know her triggers and how to intervene.

A number of years back, we had a young man thirteen years old named Isaac, placed from relative care. He really was a good kid who wanted to do well and please adults, especially teachers. One night at study time he completely blew up and was screaming, trashing his room, tearing up notebooks, breaking pencils, etc. Youth care staff came rushing to find me as they had never encountered this from Isaac, nor had I. When I entered his room he was crying on his bed and it took a while for him to tell me what was wrong.

I started the discussion by telling him the staff was concerned as he was always under control and did well in general. The staff and I felt something must be terribly wrong for him to get this riled up. Isaac confided that he knew the staff held him in high esteem and his behavior was totally different than he or we were accustomed to. He also advised me that he had figuratively "hit the wall," as he had an assignment in math he had no idea how to do. This really frustrated him and brought all of the feelings of low self-worth crushing in on him, and he blew up.

I reminded Isaac that he almost always did well in school and I was confident that with a little help he would master the new math problems assigned. I asked if he would accept some help (not from me as my math skills were deplorable, which he thought was funny), something he had never asked for in the past. Isaac agreed and I located a staff member who was very good in math who proceeded to work out a few problems then assist Isaac on the next two or three. Isaac caught on quickly and finished the assignment feeling considerably better. Neither the staff nor I addressed the blow up by Isaac until we got the math problems completed.

Once his major concern was covered, we then discussed alternatives to blowing up when feeling frustrated and stymied. Isaac confided that he had dealt with a lot of frustration in his life but tonight the math just got to him as he had always considered himself a good student. A few math problems seemed to impact his self-esteem more so than being dumped by relatives in a youth home. However, the problem with math just reinforced to him his relatives' opinion of him as being worthless. The math problem was the proverbial "straw that broke the camel's back."

This goes to show how fragile children can be, as well as how resilient. Isaac went on to foster care and, as expected, graduated with honors from high school.

The two co-regulation management techniques we utilized that evening with Isaac were concepts learned through Cornell University's Therapeutic Crisis Intervention—tremendous training for anyone engaged with young people.

The first was "hypodermic affection." The second was "hurdle help." Both are very effective when dealing with a child that is frustrated and facing new challenges or tasks they have not faced or experienced failure with in the past.

HYPODERMIC AFFECTION

This is basically what it implies, a "booster shot" of encouragement and respect when a child like Isaac acts in an uncharacteristic manner in that he was ready to surrender and give up. It is giving Isaac an "attaboy, you can do it," when his behavior may appear to call for the direct opposite. I like to call it "throwing a curve when the kid is looking for a fastball," technique. Assuring Isaac that he was a better student and person than present behavior indicated gave him the affection and respect to consider trying something else… help with homework.

Isaac was not used to asking for help and had learned to be as self-sufficient as possible in all matters. It reminds the child that we like them regardless of the behavior being exhibited, and we have confidence in him. It does not always have to be verbal in nature; it can be a pat on the back when you really want to put a foot on his rear. These "boosters" help build the relationship, and a child with a low opinion of himself needs considerable encouragement, and will begin to come looking for it from a person he trusts. Isaac and others can also take the constructive criticism and discipline if administered fairly by the person who has often given the "booster."

HURDLE HELP

With Isaac we also utilized the T.C.I. concept of hurdle help. This is simply helping the child with a new task or problem he can't seem to get over without some assistance. In Isaac's case he was frustrated over not being able to do his new math homework. Being inept in school was a new experience for him and our ability to respond with hurdle help not only helped him learn the math, but it taught him a way of getting assistance when he needs it. That particular night it was math, but the point made to Isaac when we discussed the whole episode, later, was, "Look, we all need help from time to time. It's OK not to know everything or how to handle all situations. When you are blocked or stumped, go ask for help."

Hurdle help is not enabling, it is short term and task specific. We did not turn around and do all of his homework, he did not need our help but for a few problems. We also provided hurdle help in getting his room back in shape, I picked up one broken pencil and Isaac promptly took over the remainder of the cleaning.

With Isaac it was homework that was the external "trigger" to his explosion, although feeling inadequate and inept was the internal "trigger," as it reinforced negative images his family had implanted in his mind and the trauma he had experienced, and blamed himself for, by their rejection. Isaac identified himself as a very good student, it was something he could hold on to as central to his self-perception; when he failed, his internal reaction was to see himself the way his family had, "as a loser." Can you imagine how it felt to Isaac to lose his one identifiable strength?

It would be easy to have thought or said, "Come on Isaac, what's wrong with you, it is only a stupid math question!" When in reality it was a mountain he could not climb and one he felt was falling on him!

RE-DIRECTING

Redirecting is another T.C.I. concept. It involves diverting a child's attention and focus away from an anger escalating situation onto something more pleasant and appropriate. This works well when in groups as well as for an individual. It can also be effective with Sarah when she is sad or down in the dumps. Get her up, get her out, and get her active. We know from neurological research that physical activity like exercise, walking, playing tennis, etc. gets the brain engaged in mood boosting action. These activities are great diversions and can serve to clear her mind and think more lucidly.

Diversions that work best are those things Sarah likes to do when she is feeling upbeat, if it is skating, go skating, working in a garden, go out with her and work in the garden. It always seems to have its best impact when it is a fun activity done with the adult who has the best relationship with the child. Contrary to what a lot of parents think, kids will do all kinds of fun stuff with them if they will take the initiative to get it started.

Our Recreation Director and Educational Director have repeatedly had our residents in groups as well as individually plant flowers, hike, collect rocks, sew, knit, dance, (picture thirteen kids in a dining room with our staff all doing the Brazilian Zoomba dance), play Twister, work puzzles, etc. When we discuss this with parents, they think we are crazy as they never believed their kids would do those things. When new ideas for such activities come up I am almost always the skeptic who in the back of his mind is thinking, "No way will they get this group to do that." And to date I have been proven wrong each and every time. Give it a try, see what happens, I think you, like I, will be surprised.

Another tried and true method to assist Sarah in improving self-control and regulation of emotions is the cognitive behavioral approach of:

STOP, LOOK, AND LISTEN

During your discussion with Sarah you can introduce the above as a technique that adults and other children use when needing to exert self-control. Stopping, coming to a complete standstill, helps us exert self-control. I am no longer moving, I am at rest, I am beginning to take control of my physical being, I am shutting down my body and my mouth, I am listening to my body talk to me, I am biting my tongue, I am placing my hands where they cannot easily strike out, and I am taking deep breaths or short panting breaths (like an overheated dog) to cool down.

Looking, gives me a chance to see clearly what is really going on. I see and gather facts. I look for people who might be of help. I give myself time to be sure I am seeing what is really taking place. As I look I talk to myself about what it is I see, I ask myself questions about the environment I am in.

Listening helps me make sense of what I see and feel. I tune in to my better inner voice, the one of reason, control, and maturity. I listen for positive external voices of friends, teachers, counselors, parents. I listen to my own calming down cues, telling my body and mind to relax and chill out.

As I do all three I allow time to come up with the best possible response available.

Whatever it is you are doing, simply STOP!

Visualize the big red STOP sign!

Don't DO anything!

Don't SAY anything.

FEEL your body talk to you, the tenseness, flushing, heat, cramping.

Control your body; put your fists in your pockets or behind your back. Bite your tongue. Use backward counting.

STEP ON YOUR EMOTIONAL BRAKES!

BREATHE! BREATHE! BREATHE! Deeply, bring in the good air and push out the old!

LOOK!

Use your eyes, see what is happening. Recognize the immediate environment. Ask yourself…

"Am I exaggerating?"

"Am I overreacting?"

"What is present that can help me?"

"Am I seeing things clearly?"

LISTEN!

To your inner voice, "the good one," the one that reminds you how to act. To external voices that assist and help, teachers, friends, parents...

Use proper "self-talk," tell yourself cues to chill out, calm down, get over it!

Utilizing the Stop, Look, and Listen system involves a few skills needing further explanation, especially if you are going to model and "teach" them to Sarah.

LISTENING AND FEELING YOUR BODY

When we escalate, get angry, frustrated, or emotional in any sense we have physiological reactions. As mentioned before often these body messages can serve as early warning indicators of coming disruption or explosion. An increase in pulse, flushing of the face, sweating, clammy palms, tightness in the chest, clenching of fists, tightening of muscles, cramps... are all messages our body is sending to our brain telling the brain of the stress being felt. We need to explore with Sarah what messages or early indicator warnings her body sends, and how to use such to respond prior to exploding or imploding.

BREATHING

Teaching a child how to breathe when under stress can be a wonderful gift to give a child. Taking a deep cleansing breath or two or three can help Sarah release old pent up air and feelings, while bringing in fresh, clean air. We know that good air in and bad air out is a cooling off technique in animals and humans. We also know, thanks to natural childbirth—Lamaze classes—concentration on breathing can take away the focus on pain and stress. Lamaze teaches both the cleansing (deep) breathing and the panting method, like a dog, just not as pronounced. Using either gives us time to consider how we might respond, brings in good air, blows out the bad, and interrupts our focus on the stress or trigger. I have had considerable success with children following a physical restraint utilizing the cleansing deep breaths as a way of beginning the "recovery phase" from an intense physical encounter.

BITING THE TONGUE

I highly recommend we teach this skill, and better yet practice such routinely. As I have told a number of children and adults I work with, "I have never gotten into trouble by keeping my mouth shut. Never!" One way to keep my mouth shut when I so desperately want to open it; is to simply try to curl my tongue and clamp my teeth on it. I cannot easily curl my tongue, so this takes a little concentration. Putting it between my teeth keeps my message, if it comes out at all, garbled. It is also easy to demonstrate and can provide a humorous experience when discussing with Sarah.

BACKWARDS COUNTING

Make sure you emphasize the need to count back from a relatively high number. Counting forward is too easy, routine, and fast. Start at 100 and count back by 2's... try it, and see if you don't have to concentrate. The concentration on this task relieves stress and puts the focus on the skill not the trigger, as well as giving us time to calm down. It makes our "thinking brain" work rather than our "feeling brain" being dominant. Be sure when you discuss this with Sarah that you go first and model the skill.

POSITIVE IMAGERY

I have had more difficulty teaching this skill to children than the others. It is not as difficult to teach, as it is difficult to get the child to buy into. Coming up with a positive, pleasing, calming image or place in Sarah's mind she can go to when upset can be very helpful to her. It takes practice as the mind is overriding this positive image with images of how it would feel or look if she exploded, which can often be more enticing than her own "happy place." Providing a place of refuge can be of assistance, especially in your home. "Sarah your bedroom is your safe haven. When you get upset you can go there and shut the door if needed."

If Sarah has some place else to go... go for it, she is more apt to calm down if she picks and chooses the place to do so.

A friend of mine in high school had many difficult family issues to deal with. When it became too much he would come to my house and suggest we walk back to a lake about a mile's hike. We would go there and skip rocks for an hour or so, saying very little except to comment on the occasional great rock or throw that skipped one all the way across. We did not talk about the recent fight at home or drunken stupor of his dad last night. He just went to his "happy place" and took me along for company. Hopefully you and Sarah can at some point find a similar "lake" and activity that works for all.

As for the happy place in her mind, that can be much more difficult as children who have experienced trauma may not have a "happy place," and going into the recesses of their minds might be more provoking and trauma producing. I suggest exploring a "real" place first so you can use that as a point of reference, before expecting a child to do such internally.

NEGATIVE IMAGERY

I try not to be a negative person – I prefer to keep the positives out front and believe rewards motivate people, especially young people, more so than consequences.

However, from time to time it is necessary to have Johnny or Sarah "conjure up" a Negative image to remind him/her as to what could be lost.

To illustrate, I work with quite a few young people who have been adjudicated delinquent and the Court has placed them at our agency as a last chance to avoid the Department of Corrections (DOC). Some of these kids struggle to find or envision a "happy place." But they can respond to imagery that evokes a "not so happy place." When engaged with that young person I ask him to ask himself what happens if I violate a Court rule or order? Is it worth it? He knows the positives of such behavior, be it staying out past curfew with his friends and having fun, or smoking marijuana to get a "buzz," but too often he does not ask what is the negative.

The question I pose is, "Johnny, is getting high Friday night with your buddies worth a six month placement a hundred miles away from your family and friends locked down in the DOC?" It is a very negative image, indeed, that resonates, especially if Johnny has spent just one Friday night in secured detention.

As I remind the youngsters I work with, I seldom have gotten into a jam after considering the negative outcomes or from saying "No", but have often gotten myself into trouble by going for the immediate gratification and feel good moment or saying "Yes" too soon. Both sides need to be considered.

GRANDMA ON MY SHOULDER

This is a take-off on the old cartoons where the angel pops up on the character's shoulder to whisper good advice in one ear while the devil pops up on the other shoulder to give the bad advice, playing to the character's selfish motives.

I call it Grandma on My Shoulder as most of the kids I have known have a favorite relative, usually a Grandma who they love and who loves them. I ask the youngster before they act to stop, look on their right shoulder, and imagine Grandma sitting there. What would she want to see you do and what would she want to say to you? Would the choice you are about to make leave her feeling proud and happy, or would it make her disappointed, scared, and hurt?

If Grandma on your right shoulder can't convince you of what to do, look on your left shoulder and imagine the Judge sitting there and ask the same questions?

The Grandma image seems to evoke more critical thinking than the Judge, and it is a worthwhile skill to help a young person develop.

The above mentioned are all skills you can practice, share, and teach Sarah as they will assist her in making improved, healthier, more rational, and effective responses.

The last thing on the Stop, Look, and Listen method is this… HER BEST RESPONSE.

Once she has used the Stop, Look, and Listen, she still may have to respond in some manner. You may help her formulate alternatives, but the final response is all hers.

If the response is still negative and harmful, try to get reconsideration for the next time, but endorse her use of the Stop, Look, and Listen method. It most likely resulted in a better response than the usual. Assure Sarah during your discussion that she can come up with improved responses and reactions, and that this method provides her the opportunity and time to do so.

We can help Sarah exert improved self-control by increasing her emotional vocabulary, as discussed throughout this book. Below are feelings that Sarah and other children perceive as anger. If we can help them modify their talk, we can help them modify their self-talk, and reactions/behavior. Example: If I am "angry" then I am justified in striking out. If I can modify my self-talk to tell myself I am frustrated, I have a better chance of coming up with an alternative behavior that is more appropriate for the feeling I am experiencing.

Feelings that are often confused as being anger…

abandoned, aggressive, annoyed, anxious, argumentative

betrayed, bitter, burdened

cheated, combative, confused, crushed

defeated, destructive, disappointed, discontented, dissatisfied

distraught, disturbed, disgusted

emotional, enraged, exasperated, embarrassed

fearful, flustered, frantic, frustrated, fussy

gloomy

hard headed, hard hearted, hateful, headstrong, helpless, horrible, hostile, hurried

ignored, impatient, imposed upon, infuriated, intolerant, irritable

jumpy

mad, miserable

naughty

obnoxious, outraged, outspoken, overwhelmed

pained, panicked, persecuted, petrified, pressured

quarrelsome

rattled, rejected, resentful

scared, screwed up, spiteful, stubborn, sulky

tense, trapped, temperamental, troubled, threatened

unfriendly, unkind

vindictive, violent

worried

It is amazing what children will tell themselves, i.e. the "self-talk" which is so often negative and far from the truth.

This is especially true with adolescent females, who struggle with identity, who she is, who she wants to be, who society says she should be, who her friends want her to be, who her parents think she is, on and on.

No wonder at times Sarah seems to be four different people in a two hour period. The "true" Sarah seems to get lost, with only glimpses.

Trying to please all puts tremendous strain on a young girl's psyche and often she will respond emotionally, including being depressed and exhibiting suicidal thoughts and gestures much more so than her male counterpart.

Mary Pipher in her book *Reviving Ophelia, Saving the Selves of Adolescent Girls* does an excellent job addressing these issues. This book is a little dated (1994) but from my experiences with these girls it still rings true.

It is interesting, and a little frightening to note, that the young ladies of late seem to manifest these feelings more aggressively and externally than before. They are more open to anger outbursts and violence, with less and less internalization... much like the adolescent male.

Although this seems to be a trend with the girls, boys who are depressed or sad seem to show this in a more external mode. Where Sarah tends to INTERNALIZE her sadness...

Johnny's is seen in his frustration and striking out (EXTERNALIZED), and this is one of the reasons boys are at times not diagnosed appropriately.

Johnny does not want to admit being sad, as being sad, blue, or depressed is a feminine malady. He has little problem being seen as a "bad guy" or "tough case" or "oppositional and defiant," all of which can be the result of internal thoughts and feelings of sadness and confusion.

There have been a number of occasions where I have sat with a psychiatrist and adolescent male and heard him deny over and over being sad, but readily admit to his hostility, easily frustrated, and generally "pissed off" without being able to target a reason for such behavior. I have experienced more boys refusing to take an anti-depressant than any other psychotropic.

When working with Johnny, it helps to explain his feelings in a different form than using the words "depressed or sad." Again, such a blanket statement literally "covers" the child in a "smothering tarp" from which he will struggle to escape, rather than an acknowledgement of a feeling that can be modified and improved with different choices and decisions.

Remember, children see a diagnosis as a way of being … "I'm depressed." We want them to see a situation or concern as temporary and manageable with better choices, decisions, and coping skills.

Along with Piphers book another work worth reading specific to boys is Michael Gurian's *The Wonder of Boys*.

I have worked with a large number of young people and almost each and every one was referred because of "anger management issues," or "poor self-control." Hour after hour has been spent with these kids, working through their emotions and trying to increase their skills, one of which is proper identification of what it is they are truly angry or upset about.

Some of these kids have resorted to drastic measures to hide or "mask" their real emotional pain by self-infliction of physical pain, i.e. "cutters" "burners" and self- mutilation. It has been my experience that most of the children exhibiting such behavior were female adolescents, but not always.

As foreign as this may seem to you and me, a young lady cutting herself is dealing with the emotional pain by engaging in self-inflicted pain which in her brain can release the chemicals needed to feel emotionally better, as well as take her focus from emotional to physical pain.

These kids who harm or self-injure are difficult and at times seem like onions, you patiently peel away one level of pain and find the next. Don't try to go it alone with a child like that, seek professional experience and assistance. But be aware kids who work through this torment usually do so based on a relationship with a person who over time has shown them they will stick with them come hell or high water.

One such man I knew, Fred age fifteen, was both a drug user and had a two year history of alcohol abuse. He came from an extremely neglectful background and was a self-mutilator. He cut and burned himself on his forearms, using lit cigarettes or a cheap lighter.

He was not easy to work with as he, of course, did not trust anyone. Adults had hurt him in ways most people cannot imagine and he was not going to let anyone get close enough to help him because that meant that person was close enough to harm him.

Fred and I spent a lot of time together, including sitting behind a dumpster while I watched him cut his arms with a soup can lid. I was there simply to keep the cutting to a minimum, and just by being present it went from cutting to scratching, to scraping. After he was done and de-escalated, Fred asked me why I did not jump in and grab the lid can. I replied that I was there simply to keep him safe and would have done so if I felt he was truly suicidal. However, I knew he must be in some "hellacious pain" and I did not want to stop his "lesser pain" with my interference... unless absolutely necessary.

Please remember, he had no history of suicidal ideations or actions. As we talked, he related to me numerous stories of cutting and burning himself, showing me the scars (his way of letting me in a little more to his world). Over time, months, we became pretty close and he would utilize me when he felt like cutting or burning to talk out some of the pain. He agreed with my urging and support, including attendance to start back at AA and NA meetings as these had helped in the past. He met a sponsor who became a lifelong friend, and actually participated in his sponsor's wedding (this was his sponsor's first wedding ceremony in which he walked down the aisle sober) and they remained friends. Fred actually wore my dress shoes, shirt, and tie to this wedding!

Fred's self-harm gradually decreased in severity and duration at first, then in occurrence, and finally completely. He has stayed in touch over the years and has had a fairly successful life, considering his start.

When we provide care for angry and emotional children we need to remember a few basic rules...

1. First consider the trauma history, age, emotional, intellectual, and developmental stage or status of the child. A boy at age eight with autistic characteristics will probably need a different response from us than a sixteen year old young man with oppositional behavior.

2. Utilize an empathetic approach, i.e. ask yourself, "If I were Sarah, living in her world, what is it I would need and want?" It is the ability to see yourself in that child's position with that particular child's history. Also ask, "If I were Sarah, having lived her life, would this behavior seem abnormal or unusual to me?" Sometimes we tend to see things that aren't truly there only because we don't know the child or think we know everything about the child. Sometimes the child, being in the environment she is in, has us viewing things differently solely on the environment. "Well, you know she has been tossed out of four foster homes, I guess she is working on her fifth!"

3. Don't personalize the emotional behavior you are witnessing. Easier said than done (remember my experience with Kyle). But if we take Sarah's emotional actions as being our fault or directed at us personally, progress will be extremely difficult. Realize, too, that another form of personalization is expecting Sarah to "deal with" the problem like you did. Some of the experiences Sarah has had may be very similar to your own. However, how you coped and progressed (if indeed you did) may not work for her. You need to be careful working with a child who reminds you so much of "myself at that age."

4. Again, as always, deal with the FEELING not the CONTENT of the emotional message.

5. Acknowledge that the FEELING being expressed is OK; however, acting on that FEELING in an aggressive, hostile, or self-harmful way is not OK. Sarah has the right to feel anyway she wants about anything

she wants. Neither she nor you have the right to act out those feelings in a way that hurts herself or others.

6. Reward the behavior you want to see. Positive reinforcement goes a long, long way. If punishment worked, there would be very few children in out of home care or detention facilities. I have worked with children who have been "punished" and "disciplined" in unbelievable ways. Negatives can work, but only for the very short term. Obviously someone can hold a gun to our head and make us respond as he indicates, however, remove the gun and we will respond in a different manner.

7. Whenever possible, give "ownership" for the feeling, behavior, and the subsequent rewards or consequences to Sarah. Get her advice on what consequences should be, or even better what rewards she would respond to. It was, after all, her feeling and her behavior, good or not so good; she needs to "own up." If you have to impose some sort of sanction, I doubt you will be seen as 100% fair and just. However, you can take some of the onus off of your back by getting her input.

Likewise, do not take credit for her success. Whenever possible, let the "chips hit the table," i.e. let the natural consequences take effect. We learn best when we suffer the natural consequences of our behavior... they have a greater impact than logical or externally imposed consequences.

"From my experience of hundreds of children, I know that they have perhaps a finer sense of honor than you or I have. The greatest lessons in life, if we would but stoop and humble ourselves, we would learn not from grown-up learned men, but from the so-called ignorant children."
-Mahatma Gandhi

8. Be the behavior you want to see from Sarah. Again, role modeling is crucial.

Honest expression of honest emotion does not need apologizing, if an honest concerted effort is given by you. When you are upset, express it honestly in a manner you would want Sarah to use if it was her that was angry. "Doggone it! I am upset and this is how I choose to handle it." Set the example!!!

"We can do no great things, only small things with great love."
-Mother Teresa

Along with Mother Teresa's admonition I would add… with great patience, understanding, and empathy.

Chapter 7

What can I do after the emotional storm has passed?
Discussing difficult experiences.

"Beautiful and graceful, varied and enchanting, small but approachable, butterflies lead you to the sunny side of life."
-Jeffrey Glassberg

I was called in the late morning by the principal of a local school where a few of our residents attended. Just like in my days in elementary school, when the principal asked to see me, the news was usually not good. I was informed to come to the school immediately as one of our residents was being suspended for fighting.

When I arrived at the school I could see Hakeem, age 13, sitting in a chair in the office area, fists clenched, a deep scowl on his face, and his lips muttering, thankfully, under his breath.

From the principal's report Hakeem and another boy got into a fight in the hall going from gym class to his next period. This caught me by surprise for a couple of reasons. Hakeem and his brother had been in placement for over six months and I thought he had made significant progress in handling what was described to us at the time of placement as being his "hair trigger" temper, especially in school. Prior to placement at our facility he had been suspended the previous two years for fighting. However, this year he had enjoyed some success both as a student and athlete.

Another surprise was this took place in front of his physical education teacher that he liked. Hakeem enjoyed competing in gym class and usually won most contests. He had not had any issue in the class that day, but transitions/changes are almost always difficult for many kids in school, and Hakeem was no different. Apparently he got pushed from behind, more than once, and became agitated, said something, the other boy responded, and the fight ensued. Hakeem, to his credit, did respond appropriately to his teacher's intervention.

Hakeem was given a one day out of school suspension. He knew the consequences of this action in our program, he would lose off campus activities for the weekend, something he worked for and enjoyed.

Before we left the building I could see he was still agitated and quietly reminded him that we needed to leave the building without further issues. I asked him if he could accompany me, alone, or if we needed the principal? I also asked if he could leave quietly without further commenting to anyone in the hall, even if someone said something to provoke him? He responded he could and would do so, and I used some key cues for Hakeem to prompt his behavior as we left school and crossed the parking lot... "Remember, buddy, be cool, relax. At ease Hakeem, we can work this out." I did not want to fully engage him until we were in the van or back at the facility as I did not want to escalate him on school property. Even though he was with me, had he said or done something in the parking lot or school, the school would have jurisdiction.

Although I had the principal and teacher's report as to what had taken place, I needed Hakeem's perspective and viewpoint. Once we got to the van and we were buckled in, I thanked him for leaving with me as I had asked. I then began our discussion as I had a number of times with Hakeem over similar issues, looking at him and asking, "Hakeem you love gym class and Mr.___, what in the hell happened today?"

It was important to start the conversation on a positive note, thus the reminder of how he liked gym, the teacher, and was beginning to feel good about school in general. I was hoping a positive framework would entice him to open up and tell me his side of things on the short ride home.

Having a history with Hakeem and his familiarity with me and the method we had used to discuss such events in the past, it did not take much for him to talk freely. By the time we arrived back on our campus, maybe a five minute ride, he had delivered his version and was using the method described in the coming pages. We were able to complete this method/process within a few minutes of our return, including HIS plan of action for the next school day.

To his credit, Hakeem possessed good intellect and, as noted, his familiarity with how the process worked was of assistance during this discussion. With Hakeem I only had to pose the original question and he was on board and running through the other steps with minimal verbal input from me.

The method utilized by Hakeem, and a tried and true format I have used for over 25 years, is the Life Space Interview (L.S.I.) developed by Fritz Redl in the late 1940's.

The L.S.I. is a major component of the Cornell University Therapeutic Crisis Intervention Training I was first introduced to in 1983. According to Mr. Redl, the L.S.I. "is the clinical exploitation of life events." The L.S.I. is based on the concept that when a child is in crisis over a real life event, the child is most susceptible to understanding and growth from the experience with the help of an adult versed in the skill. The sooner this real life event is discussed with the parties involved, the better the chance of success, while it is still fresh on the child's mind and the need for resolution is more critical in the moment.

This is not the only process one may choose to use when discussing important real life events but it has been my experience that this format will also serve to enhance your relationship while it increases the child's skills.

The more skilled and competent a child feels, like Hakeem, the more confident he is and acting on such increases his feelings of self-worth and self-responsibility. In the numerous trainings I have conducted, I always advise new childcare staff that the best tool they can use is the L.S.I. When I get "stuck" in counseling, I go right back to the L.S.I.

As to Hakeem, he was very proud of his plan and was actually eager to return to school the next day. School was normally an environment in which he did not feel particularly competent or confident. However, past experiences with the L.S.I. plans had proven successful and therefore he thought this one would work. Two major keys with any plan like this to be successful are 1) it needs to be the child's plan and 2) he needs to "work" his investment . Those two things seldom happen when the plan is imposed from an adult, especially if that adult is seen as an authority figure.

Your child, like Hakeem, through the L.S.I. has the opportunity to learn effective coping skills, gain a better understanding of his responsibility for his behavior, and be able to "get" the connection between feelings, thoughts, and behaviors.

The steps of the Life Space Interview are as follows:

I – ISOLATE the conversation. Go to a place where you and Johnny can talk freely with minimal interruption. If it is somewhere he feels comfortable you improve the chances of having a meaningful discussion. Letting him choose the place, within reason, puts the action in his court and jumpstarts the sense of self-regulation, ownership, and self-capability. Tell Johnny that, "we need to talk" or "I need to listen to you about what just took place," and you want him to have the time and place where he can freely express himself in his own way and at his own pace so you can gain a better understanding of whatever the crisis, situation, problem, or event just took place. Many of the young people coming into your home, or our facility, have never been given such choices, options, and power. Most are used to the adults taking control and the "discussion" being conducted on their needs and goals. This first step indicates to Johnny his importance, status, and that his self-determination is important to you.

In Hakeem's episode, the place to talk was not that important. Having conducted a number of L.S.I.s with him, I sensed he needed to "unload" as soon as possible.

I have found that children who are often reluctant to sit down and do a "face to face" may be more inclined to speak freely in a car, traveling, taking a walk, listening to music, playing basketball or cards, etc. These activities give both parties something else to focus on as well as the discussion and seem to decrease the intensity of feelings. Bill, the director at our facility for over nineteen years referred to this as "windshield therapy." He felt it allowed the young person to focus on the road or task without eye to eye contact.

I knew a foster mother who referred to this as "taking the long way home." Once her children started talking she began looking for alternative routes home to extend their time to talk. She was clever at disguising her tactic and would at times drive out of her way if a favorite song of one of her children came on the radio. As would be expected, her children became accustomed to "Mom going out of her way," with such detours becoming the norm.

Growing up, the best conversations I had with my mother (a great listener and natural born counselor without degree) took place when she washed the dishes while I dried and put away. With my father it was in the car, working on a mutual chore, or at ease while fishing.

Once I went away to college we had great talks and sometimes "debates" on trips to and from school. I always enjoyed and volunteered to pick up my kids, and their friends, at college. Being patient and listening, I learned a lot and at times was actually asked for my opinion and advice. The private drives, however, were the best!

E – EXPLORE his point of view. It is vitally important for Johnny to go first. Bite your tongue and invite him to talk. You may have to start this conversation with a question, "Johnny, in your own words tell me what just happened?" Guide him along with open ended questions such as, "What was it that upset you?" Let him talk. Let him vent. You being the active listener/facilitator does not mean you agree, approve, or accept what he is saying. Help him get an idea of the order of events, to clarify and, if possible, sequence "What happened first? Who said what, when and to whom?"

After ample time, information, and the expression of his point of view, you can then step in and try to summarize what you have gleaned from his input. Focus on his feelings, his thoughts, his behaviors, and check with Johnny to see if you have gotten things straight. If not, ask him to clarify. This will be a new way of him communicating with an adult. It won't be easy and at times it will be awkward. He will need your reassurance that what he says won't be held against him in that you "asked for it." That does not mean there won't be consequences for the behavior, just not for the discussion of the event.

Oh yeah, remember… you did ask for it!

With Hakeem I thought I had a good grip on what took place, but by starting this process and letting him tell his story first, I soon found out I did not have such a grip. I discovered he did not actually fight in class or the hall, it was at recess following a very competitive gym class. He was jostled in line and had words, but the words exchanged did not become fists until the playground. This might seem a minor issue to an adult, but to Hakeem it was obviously significant. The significance came as he had been making a concerted effort to improve his self-control and be a better student. His statement to me was, "Gary, they didn't tell you right, it was not in gym." Hakeem's perception is of primary importance and he wanted to make sure I understood the facts so I could better understand his behavior. He never once asked for absolution nor did he try to rationalize his behavior… huge steps in his skills.

With Hakeem, the clarification of where the altercation took place led me to use a different approach when I came to share my view. My favorite term for this is the "reality rub in." Knowing the "facts" also helped when attempting to connect his feelings with his thoughts and subsequent behavior. Factual information from Hakeem's perspective might not be 100% true, but his facts also influenced the alternatives and plan later developed.

Let Johnny talk. Wait… your turn is coming.

S – SHARE your point of view. Now it is your turn! Keep focused on the "rub in" of reality, it is not the "pound in," "preach in," "yell in," "demand in." Visualize a soft massage of your view gradually rubbing in what you saw/were told, heard, felt, etc. into Johnny's perception. You can start the verbal massage by saying, "OK Johnny, I think I have an understanding of what you saw, felt, thought, and acted, but let me share what I saw (was told/reported if you were not present). You can also follow this by rubbing in why the subsequent behavior took place, as in Hakeem's case, "Because they saw you hit the other boy last, Mr. _____ had little choice but to suspend you."

If you were witness to the event, then speak to what you saw, heard, thought, and why you responded. This gives Johnny your perception and view as well as a reason for your behavior. He can, of course, enter into the discussion, but try to avoid the classic power struggle which often starts with the, "He said, she said" debate. You may have to gently remind him that you listened to him without interrupting or disputing his version and you need the same from him. Let Johnny know he will have plenty of time to clarify and rebut when you finish. Try to be as brief as possible. His attention span is not the same as an adult's. As you talk, new things might come to Johnny's mind and he will want to give you this new information. If that comes up and it is truly a major difference or feeling go back to E- EXPLORE, and allow him to further clarify. Do the same if you notice he is escalating or perplexed during your "rub in."

C – CONNECT the behavior with the feelings. In my opinion, this seems to be the toughest step to master, but it is essential as this is where the real growth starts by helping him connect his feelings and thoughts to his subsequent behavior. This particular episode, as well as previous such episodes, can truly help him begin to recognize his triggers, buttons, body feelings, self-talk and how all of these things directly influence his behavior.

So many of the young people I have worked with believe they have little if any control over their emotions, self-talk, and, therefore, their behavior. It is during this step that we introduce the concept that our feelings, thoughts, and self-talk are all connected to our behavior. The hope is if Johnny can see how these things relate and influence, he can begin to develop skills to gain mastery on all. The skill of self-regulation depends on one's ability to recognize the feeling, think about the feeling, correct negative self-talk about the feeling and thought, and act in a more healthy, rational, effective, and safe manner. What you are engaged in with Johnny is co-regulation. You are cooperatively helping him to regulate himself. If you can get this accomplished on one behavior, try to engage Johnny in looking at how he has had similar experiences and behaviors or might in the future... going from the specific to the general.

Connecting behavior with times, situations, people, etc. can also be helpful.

If Hakeem knows he is always "pumped up" after gym, he needs to recognize this is his time to be on alert to losing control. If Johnny always seems to have a problem with a particular person or type of person, upon recognition of such he can develop strategies to handle the situation when he comes in contact with the person again.

If Sarah is always on edge before visiting her "real" family you can discuss this with her and maybe help her mitigate those feelings and at least recognize them. Kids in general have difficulty with transitions... coming and going, new places, people, and things. Knowing this we need to assist them in handling and help structure those transitions. The same is true for "free time," that is why we see most school fights break out in halls and playgrounds, kids get louder and rowdier on the way out the door or to the bus.

In Hakeem's situation, most of the connecting was accomplished during the "reality rub in," probably due to our history. The same held true with exploring alternatives.

Hakeem did not wait to get back to campus to write down alternatives or use my grease board to list and contemplate. He blurted out three or four possible things he could have done differently, other better choices to retaliating. He regretted not thinking and utilizing these while it escalated. His comments were, "I knew better," and "Why didn't I do this on my own before getting into trouble?" I acknowledged that he was absolutely right, he did have better ideas than retaliation that probably would have resulted in a better outcome for all involved.

I also reminded him that when we get upset we tend to fall back on our old habits and ways of dealing with stress and emotions. His comments did open the door for me to walk in and remind him of how we had discussed slowing down his reactions to verbal provocations, especially when he felt his "body" heating up and fists begin to clench (two of his physical warning signs). I was not rebuking or chastising him, but I was reminding and affirming that he does have the skills and ability to exercise such self-control. This is always a good time to remind Johnny of when you witnessed him "self-regulating" and talk about the difference that time from what happened today.

A – ALTERNATIVES. Choosing alternatives, for me, was the "fun" step of the L.S.I. Normally by this step Hakeem or Johnny has regained self-control, been able to discuss what has happened, been "actively" listened to, and is ready to be engaged in thinking about other possible choices to be employed if and when (it is usually when) a similar situation develops.

The idea is to get Johnny to come up with HIS alternatives, to at least OWN the process of exploring more appropriate decisions, choices and behaviors than those chosen at the time of the episode.

I like to use a grease board, but paper will work. I advise Johnny that I am going to write down whatever comes to his mind as an alternative. I think it helps all parties focus to list alternatives, sit back, look, think, then respond. Sometimes, seeing things in black and white helps point out the strengths and weaknesses of the choices.

Our kids are visual creatures, much more so than auditory, and remembering items past 1, 2, 3 or A, B, C, can be almost impossible. It does not matter to me what his choices are or how he chooses to express them. Those choices do not have to be better, nor do they have to be choices he thinks adults would approve. They just have to be his and fit as an alternative to how he previously behaved. Without limiting his choices, Johnny can hopefully see that although his behavior could have been better, it could also have been worse.

At times, if the child is struggling with the concept of alternatives, I use the analogy of a school cafeteria. I ask Johnny to think of the school cafeteria and lunch line, getting his tray, walking through the serving area, and looking at the various food choices. Some look great, others less so, some are healthy foods, some are junk food, some he likes, and some he does not. Some items may be new and exotic or too expensive and exhaust his money. But to eat he has to make choices and then pay the price, money, gas or hunger pains, etc. The same is true when looking at behavior alternatives.

When listing these new alternatives, I list whatever Johnny says, not making comments except to ask for clarification. The only choice I rule out listing is the one he made that led to the immediate problem we have been discussing. He is apt to pick out some easy choices as well as some too difficult, expensive, or exotic. It does not matter, my task is to transcribe. After he has exhausted his choices, I then see if any obvious choices are missing and ask him if I might list them for his consideration without immediate comment. I have never had a young person turn down this offer. If Johnny has listed only positive alternatives, I usually list one choice that would have been worse.

When I list a negative alternative or two, the young person almost always asks me why I did so.

The purpose of the negative alternative is to plant the seed in his brain that although his choice was poor, he did not choose worse, which means he IS capable of making even better choices in the future. In fact, as I would explain to him, he had made a better choice as the other poorer alternatives probably flew through his mind and somewhere, somehow, he did not opt for them. Now the question or task becomes to slow down even more when upset so you can come up with good responses in a bad situation. Slowing down the thought process is in itself a coping skill that leads to a choice of a better coping skill.

When we have listed the choices, I give Johnny a colored marker and I take a different color (let him make the choice) and he circles what he thinks are three of the best alternatives, and I do the same once he has finished. We then sit back some distance, look at the circles, and ask

154 The Scream of the Butterfly

each other why we circled what we circled. It is always an interesting process.

As I explain to him, I am just his consultant, it is his life, his choices, his decisions to make, his plan to put together and work, so he has to decide what to try, and what to discard at this time. An analogy is building a house, being the architect or designer, not the owner, the plan is never fully realized until the owner says so and has given all possible input.

Then we get to the "How might these choices be put in a plan, and how might they work when implemented?" part of our discussion.

P – PLAN and PRACTICE. This is the next step and fairly easy once you have his alternatives. I want to know what he thinks will work best and in what sequence i.e., "Johnny what do you think you should do first, second, third, etc?" "What has the best chance of success?" "What can you do if this plan or alternative does not work?" "What other resources are available?" Once the plan is devised and written on the board to reinforce, it is time to practice and rehearse.

Set up a similar scenario/episode, play your role, and have Johnny be Johnny and then "walk" him through his plan in a practice mode. If the practice walk through indicates he will not or can not follow the plan, then scrap it and go back to the alternative seeking step. These practices need to be very basic and demonstrated in a step by step process. To help him through it, you might offer to be Johnny first so he can see how this might look without having to do it... you are modeling the skill. If you show me how rather than tell me how, I will have a better understanding simply by my having observed the skill.

E – ENTER and RE-ENTER. Now comes crunch time and the testing of the plan. It is important, once you have completed and rehearsed the plan, to get Johnny back into the normal routine. It is common for him, just like most of us human beings, to want to avoid or evade going back into the environment where he experienced the problem. Get him back to that environment with your physical presence, be it school, playground, dining room, church, neighborhood park, whatever. Remind him you will be present while he gets comfortable, you can be reached to for assistance, and that he has developed a good plan, so rely on it. Before he re-enters, remind Johnny that you will get with him to see how the plan worked and if it did not to help him make modifications.

Hakeem had also agreed to re-enter the school setting the next morning in the usual manner and did not take me up on the offer to drive him to school and walk in with him. He did not feel such steps were necessary, nor did I, but it was my way of offering tangible support. He expressed confidence in his plan and abilities, at least until playground time, when he asked for my presence.

A word of caution with plans… be sure everyone germane to the situation is aware of the plan. I called the school and spoke with the assistant principal, who in turn relayed the essence of Hakeem's plan to the teachers involved, including the playground supervisor.

It was interesting to note that by including the school personnel they became more aware of how hard Hakeem had been working on his behavior and academics. This was the first year of middle school where he was on target to complete without being expelled. They felt he had an investment in the school, his education, and getting along with staff and peers, as well as being more effective in managing his emotions. Within a few weeks, his gym teacher (who had complained the loudest and longest about Hakeem, although Hakeem liked him), became his strongest advocate.

Sometimes such a change can take place simply by letting the adult know how he is viewed by the young person. I suppose it is human nature to "like" someone who "likes" you, as I have seen this happen a number of times with the phenomena going both ways… adult to child, child to adult. As the relationship between Hakeem and the gym teacher improved, so did Hakeem's behavior, therefore his standing improved with the teacher, and as so often happens, Hakeem's behavior continued to improve, a positive cycle.

The Life Space Interview methodology afforded Hakeem a means of expressing himself and coming up with alternatives and plans, self imposed, rather than adults handing down suspensions, restrictions, and consequences, usually with no plan of action, except to tell Hakeem, "Don't do it again or else." When we engage a child in this mode we become more of a "coach" or "mentor," rather than authority figure. We also reinforce his personal power to control his emotions, behavior, and ultimately his life.

If you look at the first letters in each step of the L.S.I. it reads…

I

E

S

C

A

P

E

You do escape, as does the child, from the snare of communication roadblocks and emotional laden responses that create a negative cycle of anger and accusation leading to more problems… the exact opposite of the positive cycle mentioned above. The L.S.I. allows both Johnny and you the opportunity to "work through" or "work out" the problem, issue, or dilemma without sinking into the quagmire of a power struggle.

For those of you parenting younger children or a child who does not have the vocabulary and conversational skills to benefit from the L.S.I.

process, Cornell T.C.I. has reworked the curriculum so that you can utilize a "streamlined" version.

There are three stages of the L.S. I. for these children…

TALK ABOUT IT

FIX IT

SMILE

The first step, "**Talk About It**," is to sit down with the child and let her talk about what took place, what she saw, how she felt, heard, etc. Unlike the older child, you may find yourself needing to ask more open ended questions to get her to talk. You then proceed by sharing, "rubbing in" your perspective. Keep it simple and focused on that particular episode or problem.

The second step is "**Fix It**" where you work with the child in coming up with better choices for the next time she faces a similar situation. Go over possible choices and decisions she may use. With a younger child or one who is developmentally delayed, I often have to prompt her thinking by giving examples of choices. Regardless of the child's age or intelligence, the choices and decisions must be hers, so be sure she makes at least one other choice.

The third step is "**Smile**." Come to an agreement on the new choices to be tried, congratulate her on her choices and the ability to sit down and talk with you, acknowledge that it can be hard to do so and takes courage. You then need to get her back to the environment or setting she came from and stay connected. A younger child will need your presence and support considerably longer than the adolescent.

You may need to be supportive through her first encounter with the issue to serve as a physical reminder of what choices she made. Be sure to check back with her more frequently and go over the choices developed… at the start of her day, at the end of the day, prior to the possibility of something coming up that would escalate her.

Cora, a young lady I worked with had similar problems in school as Hakeem. Unfortunately, she was not blessed with his intelligence and verbal skills. It was necessary for me to be more concrete in my assistance to Cora. She had been suspended one day for cussing in the hall after an argument with a boy who had a locker close to hers.

We did the above version of the L.S.I. When she returned to school the next day, some of her new choices were for me to take her to school, follow her in, hang out in the front hall/office area where I could observe both hallways while she went to her locker then on to class. As agreed, I waited twenty minutes into her first period then left the school, notifying the office personnel of Cora's new choices. My intent was to do as she asked without undue embarrassment. After school was over I picked her up and we celebrated the success of her new choices that day by going to McDonalds for a treat.

The Talk About It, Fix It, and Smile do not need to be lengthy discussions. They, too, can be conducted during a walk, activity, in a car, wherever and whenever necessary.

I prefaced my remarks to Cora with comments along these lines, "Cora I hate seeing you upset and suspended out of school. It makes me sad when you are sad. I think I know a way of making us both happier. Would you like to try it?"

Again I strongly urge you to allow your Cora to pick the place for the talk, this provides her with personal power and she will probably pick the place she feels most comfortable—a good example of structuring the environment for success.

If at first you don't succeed, try again, then try something different.

It is very frustrating for a child to be unsuccessful only to be sent back into the fray with no new skills or told to do the same thing again that has already failed!

The Cornell T.C.I. formats are outstanding in my opinion, but they do not stand alone. You may find a young person more oppositional and less willing to do the above. It is also possible that you will run up against a child who has attended numerous therapy sessions and may be what I call "therapy savvy." He or she knows what to say, when to say it, and also what not to say or reveal.

How do you engage such a child? What can you do to get him to at least "sneak a peek" at his emotions and how such impact his life?

One young man came into placement very "therapy savvy." His first comments to me during our first encounter were, "Don't pull any of that counseling crap on me. I know all of those tricks, I've seen them all." After I finished laughing, as his comments were not threatening or said in anger, I promised not to do so, and if I slipped I asked that he hold me immediately accountable.

1. PROBLEM IDENTIFICATION

I was able to engage Troy in a six step process starting with problem identification. The gist of my opening words with Troy were that he had a lot of experience in therapy, he knew himself better than I did, and since he did not want to go over the same old stuff for the 100th time, "What do you think the problem seems to be that ended with your being placed here?"

I was attempting to get his input before I offered my observations. My idea was to engage him where he felt comfortable, initially, at being engaged. My goals were to get Troy to identify a problem from his perspective, as dealing with his chosen problem or issue would hopefully get me past his denial and on the road to ownership. Children like Troy who exhibit what is usually called oppositional and defiant behavior often identify the problem in their lives as "getting caught."

Troy needed me to direct the conversations back to the consequences of getting caught, which then led to discussion of the problem behavior, what he was doing when caught. His issues and problems were very obvious to me and anyone else who would take the time to look at his history. Troy had extreme difficulty with self control and managing of his emotions. He also seemed at first to have little motivation to address this problem. Like many such young people, the lack of success in the past led Troy to doubt himself capable of any success. He felt "doomed" to struggle through life. It is perfectly normal for a young person like Troy, and especially a "trauma victim," to expect more of the same treatment, why would he expect anything else?

2. TRIGGERS AND BUTTONS

It was during this "problem identification" step that I introduced Troy to the concepts of "triggers and buttons," (as discussed in previous sections of this book Chapter 6) i.e. those things that seem to get him emotionally upset and confuses or distorts his thinking. He knew his "triggers and buttons," but had not identified them as such and this opened a torrent of information. If a child struggles with this, identify some of your "triggers" as examples and how such impact your behavior.

This helps with clarification and puts the child on notice that you, too, have similar feelings.

The actual problem he identified was getting caught after he had hit another resident in the mouth. I rephrased this as "Troy, you seem to get aggressive when you are angry, and aggression leads to consequences for you and the other boy. You get punished and the other young man has a busted lip." My next comment was, "Would you be interested in coming up with ways to avoid serving consequences?" His reply was affirmative, thinking I would simply let this episode slide. However, I countered, "To avoid consequences, we need to come up with better ways to handle those emotions than becoming physical." Once again the focus was on "how might we develop more effective coping skills that do not result in your getting into trouble?"

Troy, by using the above, was at least able to look at his behavior as problematic due to how he dealt with his "trigger" being pulled. Identifying triggers is the second step in this process.

To help him identify triggers I had to ask questions. Were these triggers internal or external, explaining briefly what I meant. I wanted Troy to identify his triggers and how when pulled he chooses to react.

Triggers being pulled ALWAYS lead to some reaction (and the vast, vast majority of the children I see that are aggressive are reacting, not proactively aggressive, i.e. premeditated). I wanted him to see that his reactions could be changed if we could get him to be proactive in regards to preventing a violent reaction so that he did not suffer consequences, hurt someone, or get hurt.

Some children will need you to add on to their observations with a few of your own. It also helps to summarize the triggers and how he chose to react. In Troy's case the comment I made was, "Troy, Dave said something nasty about your mother; you REACTED by hitting him in the mouth and busting his lip. When someone says something about your mother you don't like, that must be a trigger of yours, or is it only Dave? What other trigger do you feel was pulled? "What did you tell yourself when Dave made that comment?" All were questions leading to further discussion and identification of actions, reactions, and consequences.

3. INTRODUCTION OF INTERVENTION SKILLS.

After the above conversation I asked Troy, "What skills or tricks do you know that can help you temper your reaction when your trigger is pulled?" I was looking for Troy to define what I call a "quick fix," a skill or trick he can immediately use to, at minimum, decrease his emotional response. He was familiar with breathing techniques, backwards counting, and creating space between himself and his antagonist. So our discussion focused on his utilizing such to get through his first reaction.

When the trigger is internal, you can discuss alternative behaviors that take the focus away from the internal conflict. As previously mentioned, I advised Troy that it is a well known fact that exercise increases brain activity and hormones that stimulate an improved mood. So a child that reports feelings depressed or has an internal trigger leading to moodiness and feelings of sadness needs to get up and get moving, outside if possible and into sunshine or a physical activity.

4. REWINDING THE VIDEO/DVD.

At this point I asked Troy to rewind his video/DVD in his mind as we were going to look at what happened, as well as a possible "do over scene." I asked him to return and replay the situation immediately before he hit Dave. I had him tell me what was going on, how his body felt, what did he see, hear, smell, sense, and then act. I then asked him to hit the rewind button again, inserting his skills into the scene rather than hitting Dave. I did so to get him to "see" in his mind the utilization of these skills and alternatives to his trigger being pulled and his going off. As in Troy's case you may need to serve as his "guide" through this rewind scenario, recreating the scene and reworking the video/DVD.

Think of all of the times you wished you could have a "do over."

Young people want "do overs," too, especially when consequences have been severe. Using this step can get them to do an "imaginary do over." This can then transfer to the next "real" situation and they are more prepared.

5. REVIEWING THE ALTERNATIVE SCENARIO... THE "DO OVER" SCENE.

After coming up with other ideas and alternatives, I asked Troy to pick out the positive things he saw in the "do over" scenario that might serve as alternatives, i.e. what worked? I then did the same with the negatives, "OK Troy, what did not work?" This was done so he could give a critical look at all alternatives before putting such in place. If this endeavor did not produce alternatives he perceived as doable and viable, then it was foolish to utilize those skills.

This might sound repetitious, but a child will often give you the response they think you are looking for to please you or, as in Troy's case to get me off of his back. Looking at the positives and negatives gives the child one more opportunity to change the scenario and rework the outcome.

If the child cannot come up with "more" positive choices or alternatives, then you can step in and provide a few for consideration and go through the rewind process one more time, inserting those skills where needed. I will sometimes play the "WHAT IF GAME." What if Troy had stopped walking towards Dave; what if Troy had told himself this is just Dave trying to get me pissed; what if I had seen my child care worker in the room and asked him to intervene?

6. THINKING AHEAD.
In this step you and the child are putting a plan together to try. You want to get a commitment from the child to try the alternatives developed the next time his trigger is pulled. For any plan to work it has to be the child's, or at minimum have his honest endorsement. With Troy, I asked him to think ahead and visualize the next possible encounter (which at our facility usually came very fast upon reentering his living space) and how he might implement his alternatives and plan. If he can punch the "fast forward" button and see how the DVD might play out he is setting himself up to behave as he has "thought out" or rehearsed.

Remember, a lot of children are skeptical of their own powers and abilities. This skepticism leads to falling back on old habits and behaviors. These might be counterproductive long term but provide comfort and relief temporarily.

This format worked well with another young man, Ronnie age 14. He was very insecure and felt trapped into his patterns or behavior. He just did not believe himself capable of changing his behaviors.

Ronnie, from the first day he entered our facility, reported being picked on by an older boy. We had talked about various ways of handling "bullying" behavior, but his inclination was to immediately fight back. If the reactive aggression did not stop the "bullying," he would then become proactive in his aggression.

One of the reasons he was placed, ironically, was he was perceived as a "bully," and had engaged in planned aggressive behavior towards classmates. If Ronnie could not fight you immediately or you happened to be the victor, he engaged his intellect, which was above average, and devised a means to retaliate without direct confrontation.

Our discussion centered on the "bully," who was an older, bigger youth who he could not fight face to face with any hope of winning. As he talked, it became evident that Ronnie was figuring out a way to retaliate when the "bully" was sleeping. Unless I could engage him to use his smarts in a different and less violent manner, it was only a matter of time until he launched his "sneak attack."

Ronnie was fully aware that such behavior would not be tolerated and if he chose to do so he would seal his immediate fate... placement in a secured, locked facility, probably in the Department of Corrections.

As to his threat to get the other boy when sleeping, I chose not to react by warning or chastising him. My response was, "OK Ronnie, let's say you do carry out this sneak attack, what would be the positives and what would be the negatives just for you? Do the positives outweigh the negatives?"

I attempted to introduce the idea of the positives and negatives for his intended victim, an attempt to build some semblance of empathy for his victim. His other therapists had stated Ronnie lacked empathy, and, as expected, he was considerably more interested in his negatives and his positives rather than concern for his "bully."

From this we discussed possible alternatives, utilizing staff, maintaining distance from his antagonist, confronting the "bully" with other adults available, having the staff confront the "bully," and the general idea of being assertive. After an explanation of assertive behavior and rehearsals he agreed to try this approach. It did not force him to be aggressive but also did not make him look weak.

For the first few days Ronnie used his assertive skills and these seemed to work. However, the other boy continued to intimidate verbally and during a recreational activity, words led to blows and Ronnie and I went back to the counseling "drawing board," to come up with other alternatives. This time he was less inclined to work with me as during the fight he held his own with the bully and was almost eager to "fight it out" again, man to man (which was an improvement over a sneak attack at night).

Utilizing Step 6 eventually led Ronnie to a candid discussion, which included a more realistic look at possible responses, including the pros and cons of each.

The major con he kept coming back to was the very possible placement in the D.O.C. if and when caught. He was correct in his assessment and getting caught was a given as he had confessed to me before the act!

Ronnie at first thought it might be worth it as the striking back had felt good. I acknowledged those feelings he held as being possible positive ones, but as we worked through the consequences, he slowly began to realize he needed to develop a different strategy... not for the sake of the bully... but to save his own hide. He also had concerns as to the impact on his mother if he was placed outside of his home community in "prison." We talked about what he thought life inside a correctional facility might be like, would there be more bullies with which to contend? The distance issue with his family came up too. I encouraged him to be totally selfish, not for just a few minutes to exact his immediate revenge, but what about when that moment and feeling passed? How would he feel then?

At no time was Ronnie elated with his alternatives or plans. At no time did he stop thinking about revenge. At no time did he buy into the rights or feelings of the bully. At no time did he voice concerns about what was "morally" or "ethically" right. He did, however, show some empathy for his family and the grief and trouble his incarceration would bring to their doorstep.

Ronnie came to accept and grudgingly implemented the alternatives and plans as such behavior allowed him to deal with the bully in a manner acceptable to the Court and did not constitute a violation of his probation.

He truly wanted to wait for this boy to go to sleep, creep into his room and beat him. He agreed not to do so, to continue using his assertive skills with staff's encouragement, and requested that I speak with the other boy. Ronnie wanted the other young man to know that he did not fear him and was only going along with the plan to stay out of the Department of Corrections. He also requested that I advise the other boy that Ronnie could easily change his mind and retaliate if the bullying continued.

Upholding my end of the agreement/plan, I did meet with the other boy and communicated Ronnie's message in the words Ronnie desired. His message left little doubt in the other boy's mind. In fact, the bully was unaware just how upset Ronnie was and had grossly underestimated his ability and willingness to strike back. The bully, fully informed, decided it was wise to modify his behavior towards Ronnie and maintain a reasonable safe distance until both had completely cooled off.

Ronnie's motivation to change was based on self preservation (the same reason I stopped smoking cigarettes in 1977, I wanted to live a full life). He realized, with help, that acting on his emotions would lead to dire consequences that were not worth it. He did not "buy in" to the socially appropriate approach of assertiveness; his "buy in" was his avoidance of the consequences of a D.O.C. placement.

There are times and young people like Ronnie when this is the best you can hope and work towards. It is at least a place to start. My hope was if Ronnie tried to be assertive and avoided violence it may work and he could learn to utilize such coping skills in other situations, avoiding the altercations that had plagued his life to date.

This was not my first rodeo, and I realized it would take more than one successful episode for Ronnie to truly "buy in." Let's face it, skepticism, and at times resistance, is the norm when anyone contemplates changing an old familiar way of doing things to a new behavior. I looked for and worked towards small incremental steps of progress by Ronnie. I felt if he confronted the bully face to face and fought, that was an improvement over a sneak attack at night on a defenseless sleeping enemy. My hope was that he would not have the opportunity to fight or attack prior to having more opportunities to test out his new skills. Nothing breeds success more than success itself!

Ronnie was not the usual young person I work with, as most are "reactive" in their aggression and not "proactive." However, Ronnie's life had been one in which he was ready to "strike first" when he perceived a threat, and to think ahead and actually "plan" his behavior when and if the threat appears real or imminent... in his mind.

When you are not sure what to do to be helpful, try following these few simple steps.

1) Ask Johnny what are the things that disturb, frustrate, or tend to make him very angry (his triggers and buttons)?

2) Ask Johnny how he knows he is getting angry/frustrated/upset... what does his body feel like? Teeth clenching, butterflies in the stomach, flushing, sweating, heart racing? These are all important indicators for him to know so he can apply his skills.

3) Ask Johnny what has worked well for him in the past, what might not have worked, and what he thinks he might do with your assistance when he becomes upset?

4) Ask Johnny what it is he wants you to do when he becomes escalated? Does he need to be left alone, talked with, taken for a walk, engaged in another activity, etc.? This is important as what he wants you to do is probably going to work best for him in the immediate timeframe.

Behavior can stop, but we cannot stop behaving. When we, like Ronnie, stop an old behavior, something has to step into that void, a new behavior. Ronnie's aggressive behavior was temporarily halted, only because he had a new behavior, assertiveness, to utilize... filling the void of violent behavior. We as a staff provided positive reinforcement of and support for the new behavior. Our support and reinforcement (the fertilizer and water needed to grow new skills/behavior) were important, but it was Ronnie who did the hard work.

CHANGE AIN'T EASY!!!

If you have had an ongoing relationship with a young person or considerable experience working with children talking about goals and objectives, you may choose an approach based on William Glasser's Reality Therapy.

This is a four step approach that Glasser points out works best when we can get Johnny to use it for himself when conflict or emotional distress is first felt. By asking four key questions, this approach can serve as a way for Johnny to make a better decision or choice involving his emotions and responses.

As with most of the skills we use, we need to also transfer these to Johnny by taking the opportunity to "teach."

The first of the four questions is...

1) "WHAT IS YOUR GOAL?" Johnny might rephrase this question as "What is my goal?" The point of the question is to remind Johnny of his stated goals and objectives formerly expressed in previous discussions. If he has not done so, then the point is to get him to look at and define his goals and objectives. Questions to stimulate his thinking are "What is it that you WANT? What is it that you NEED?"

2) "STOP AND THINK, WHAT ARE YOU DOING NOW?" Johnny's question to himself would be, "What am I doing now?" You want Johnny to look at the behavior he is exhibiting, and/or the choices (decisions) being made at that instant. If you were posing the question after the episode, you would ask, "Johnny how were you behaving/ doing? What do you remember feeling? What messages were you giving yourself? How did you respond or act?"

3) "IS WHAT YOU ARE DOING HELPING YOU REACH YOUR GOAL OR OBJECTIVE? IS WHAT YOU ARE DOING HELPING YOU GET WHAT IT IS YOU WANT OR NEED?" This works best if Johnny can ask himself those questions before acting or reacting. "Will this help me reach my goal? Does this help me get what I REALLY want or need?" You may need to remind Johnny, in a non-critical manner, what his stated goals and objectives were. "Hey Johnny, you have always had the goal of graduating from high school, does this get you closer to that accomplishment or further away?"

4) Based on his response you can then ask "IF YOU DID NOT GET CLOSER TO YOUR GOAL WHAT MIGHT YOU DO DIFFERENTLY IN THE FUTURE?" If Johnny has a mistaken impression he actually moved closer to his goal with negative behavior, you will need to go back and have him reconsider the positives and negatives of his behavior. One way of doing this is to pose these two questions; "Thinking back on it, what did you do that you felt was positive or helpful? OK, now what might you have improved on or done better?" Your goal with Johnny is to get him to use this process for himself to evaluate and assess his responses, then plan for future situations, so he does improve his behavior which moves him closer to his achieving his goal.

When I first start working with a young person I usually pose this question for consideration, "Hey think for a minute about this. If you had what you truly wanted in life, what is it that you would have?" Seldom has this question failed to get an answer that has moved the discussion in a fruitful manner.

I ask the question very early in my contact as I want the young person to pause and consider, as well as to introduce him to the concept of setting goals and objectives.

I have received various responses, all interesting. Some of the answers are... money, fame, independence, to be left alone, popularity, an education, talent, respect, a good job someday, but the overwhelming response I have received is, "I want to be home."

The only stipulation I place on the answer to this question is that the goal must be something that can be obtained in the here and now or future. As much as we might want to rewrite history, we do not have that power. My proposal is that he DOES possess the power to shape and determine his future. However, I note, to shape and determine his future it will take purposeful behavior, some assistance from the adults in his life, and planning.

"The best way to predict your future is to create it." -Abraham Lincoln

Once I get a stated goal, regardless of what it is, then I can focus in on what the child needs to do to accomplish this goal. If I know for a fact that the total power is not his as to the goal, I discuss that up front. However, I also remind him that his behavior is the only thing he can control and to reach whatever goals or objectives he has will depend mostly on him.

One young man who happened to be fairly bright, talented, and articulate, responded to my question with, "I want to be a big time pimp, like in Chicago or Detroit." I don't know if he truly did or was trying to get a reaction from me. Regardless I responded, "Great, you have a goal, now what do you and I have to do so you have the opportunity to reach that goal? What do you think it takes to be a big time pimp in a city like Chicago?"

After his initial shock at my comments, we talked, and he decided there were certain things he would need and have to do to reach this dubious goal. He had just turned sixteen so he knew he had a couple of years to prepare. He also realized he could not run such an operation from a residential facility in southwest Indiana, so his first objective was to get out of our program and eventually the city. With a little nudging from me, he stated he would have to get a little older, stronger, learn more about the city he chose to go to, as well as money management, and improve his interpersonal relationship skills so he could effectively recruit and handle his "stable of ladies."

I was not being flip with this young man. If that was his goal, I could help him get there if he was willing to commit to doing those things necessary to move him down the road to what he saw as success.

The crucial point of this discussion was to get him thinking about goals, and all of the self-effort that goes into achieving anything he truly wants. To be the pimp he wanted to be he would be required immediately to start exercising better self-control, stay out of minor hassles and problems, and work through and complete our program to be released.

With this young man I was fairly confident he had the ability to be many things in life, all above the level of a pimp. However, he lacked motivation at the time to be any of those other things and needed to formulate a goal that he saw worth his hard work. I was also confident that he would, during this process of hard work, discover success and positive residuals that would lead to the development of more socially acceptable goals and life plans. After all, you don't have to be a superstar to rise above the level of a pimp!

As I later learned from him, he had decided on the life of a pimp as he had seen it done locally, felt it was within his abilities, and perceived the pimp as having money and standing in his community. He really wanted to be someone who others looked up to and envied so he pursued the life of the "role model" he had observed.

When you are engaging your young person in such a discussion, avoid getting caught up in the quality of the goal, just hold his feet to the fire utilizing the above process. If your Johnny has a certain teacher he does not like and wants to "get even", start the discussion with the idea of, "OK, let's see if we can devise a plan where you get even without getting hurt or penalized. What would really get Mr. ___'s goat!" As this is discussed you keep moving the ideas to the most appropriate, as anything negative towards Mr. ___ will result in consequences for Johnny.

Brad was a fourteen year old in placement with us who had numerous issues and concerns. However, in early conversations he had formulated a couple of immediate goals he could reach while in placement. His goals were more free time, increased phone privileges, family visits, allowance, and activities. He especially wanted to achieve the highest citizenship ranking level, which would afford him the opportunity to leave our campus for a thirty minute non-supervised walk.

His major objective, however, was to increase visitation time with his mother. He felt responsible for a younger brother who lived with her and wanted to be there for his brother. I chose to accent the positive and complimented him on his feelings of family responsibility. We discussed what he needed to accomplish during the week so his visit time could be extended on the weekend (family visits and contacts were always allowed but his behavior as well as Court stipulations could determine the length and setting for those visits).

Unfortunately, late one week he came home ill from school with the flu. As our policy required at the time, he was to be in his room most of that time to decrease the chances of the other boys on his dorm getting sick. Brad chafed at this quarantine period and was quickly violating his room restriction, causing conflicts with his staff. When I intervened I asked him, "Brad what is happening here, what is going on?"

He explained his perception with some indignation. I then asked him, "What goal have you been working so hard for this week?" He knew and replied, "Going home to see my family." My response was, "OK, is coming out of your room agitating staff getting you closer to this goal or putting it at risk? Think for yourself, are you helping Brad or hurting Brad? If you are at risk of losing some of your visitation time over this room issue, is it worth it? If not, what can you do? What can we do to help you?"

Once he started thinking along these lines he was much more amenable, as was staff, to think of a plan of action that would work for all parties to get through the one evening of quarantine. As could be expected, Brad did not quit arguing about the unfairness of the rule (and maybe it was), but I continued to shift the focus back to his goal... in effect holding his feet to the fire he started.

Brad, like all of us, is responsible for his behavior. To keep him looking at his goals also kept him focused on his behavior. I also wanted our staff to focus on his overall behavior and concerns so we did not overreact and cause more harm. But the bottom line was, if he chose to push the issue, he would be choosing to make the issue bigger than it needed to be and eventually forfeit some of his visit time. The responsibility for his behavior was on him, our responsibility was to help him work through his choices to a better result.

We cannot expect success every time, regardless of which process or method we use. The above mentioned methods are not foolproof but I have found them to be the most effective to date with young people who are angry, hurting, emotionally charged, and have suffered trauma. I believe they work best when the adult engaged has a caring and supportive relationship with the young person. Such relationships and interventions empower the child (real power is not something he is familiar exercising) to take responsibility for his own affairs and behavior.

"Too often we underestimate the power of a touch, a smile, a kind word, a listening ear, an honest compliment, or the smallest act of caring, all of which have the power to help turn a life around."
- Leo Buscaglia

Chapter 8
How do I provide effective discipline for Sarah?

"The butterfly counts not months but moments and has time enough." -Rabindranath Jagore

This will not be a diatribe, one side or the other, as to the "spare the rod spoil the child" debate or whether corporal punishment is necessary in the raising of a socially responsible well behaved child. My philosophy is not important nor is it relevant. However, without sounding pretentious, neither is yours.

When we are engaged in substitute parenting, be it foster, step, relative, whatever, we can basically rule out physical means as well as "punishment" in general. As in the case of the word "attitude" we are better off dropping it from our vocabulary. Punishment will not work when we are parenting someone else's child. In reality, being punitive with any child has, at best, a very short positive effect on the child's behavior and is counterproductive in most cases.

If punishment and physical means worked, neither you nor I would see the number of children in out of home care that we do. Children like Sarah have suffered horrific punishments and abuse... without a positive change in the behavior targeted. Punitive measures have little positive impact on the behavior, as more often than not it is the child herself, not the a specific behavior that is the target for the punishment.

Regardless, Sarah is not your child. What might have been effective with your own children is of little if any importance. The time constraints we operate under with being "substitute parents" rules out the application of discipline techniques that we might have found productive with our own children, including the occasional "swat across their bottoms."

The actual productiveness of such techniques may not have been all that effective with our own children. Recent conversations with my grown children have indicated, surprisingly to me, that some of the things my wife and I tried with them had very little immediate and almost no long term effects. Some of the things we did or said that we felt were of little consequence actually made a huge impact. We were not big believers in spankings, and it was used very sparingly, as we remember. Our children, however, have different memories and recollections, giving them a slightly different perspective on our discipline techniques.

"All is perspective; to a worm, digging in the ground is more relaxing than going fishing!"
-Clyde Abel

In your role as a "substitute parent" keep the word "discipline" at the forefront of your thoughts. Along with discipline keep focusing on "self-discipline".

Given the short time she might have in your care and the history she has, how can you help Sarah become more self-disciplined?

"Discipline, like the bridle in the hand of a good rider, should exercise its influence without appearing to do so; should be ever active, both as a support and as a restraint, yet seem to lie easily in hand. It must always be ready to check or pull up as occasion may require; and only when the horse is a runaway should the action of the curb be perceptible."
-Author unknown

The root word of discipline is disciple, with discipleship being a voluntary act. A disciple turns away from his old way of living and accepts a new way of life, new behaviors that are often extremely different from his old way of doing things. In our culture, when we think of disciples the first followers of Jesus come to mind. Those twelve men radically changed their entire lives and behaviors to accept a new way of living, relating to each other, others, and their spiritual beliefs.

This is very similar to what you want Sarah to engage in, giving up old ineffective and unhealthy ways of behaving and engaging in more rational, healthier ways of living.

One of the new ways you want to see her adopt is self-discipline, generated from within, rather than forced or coerced from without. Self-discipline is internally driven and as such is going to last longer and be more effective than punishment or other external disciplinary techniques.

Call it what you may, a "life skill," or a "coping skill," we all recognize that people do better who exert discipline on themselves than those who must be disciplined externally.

Self-discipline is not easy to teach and it is difficult for most children to incorporate into their beings. It requires teaching and modeling by the adults in the child's life.

It also requires you as the parent to hold the child accountable for her behavior so she can learn more appropriate ways of behaving.

How do you do this?

You need to be cognizant of the child's age, maturity, and developmental functioning as all will impact your efforts to instill self-discipline. It is also important to know the child's trauma history, as sending a young person to calm down in a bedroom might not be wise for her if that is where she was sexually molested. You are not going to discipline a fourteen year old as you would a two year old. It is important that the discipline methods you utilize "fit" the youngster with whom you are working.

"Rules and laws should be like clothes, tailored to fit the person wearing them."
-Clarence Darrow

As previously stated in this book, good questions to ask yourself when Sarah is acting out or "misbehaving" are...

"What purpose is this behavior serving?"

"What need is being met with this behavior?"

You cannot formulate a decent response until you have given consideration to the questions regarding the goal, purpose, and/or reason for the behavior being exhibited.

I am not a big fan of "do not's" I prefer "do's." However, there are some definite things you "do not" want to "do."

DO NOT...

JUMP TO CONCLUSIONS

EXAGGERATE

When we are upset we tend to escalate and exaggerate. Cooler heads need to prevail and you cannot expect Sarah's to be the cooler head. Refrain from maximizing the behavior, making it into something it is not. A lit match does not become a forest fire without considerable wind/oxygen/hot air fanning the flame!

RETALIATE

Retaliation only starts a negative cycle of revenge and further retaliation. When we strike back in anger or the heat of the moment, be it physically or emotionally, we initiate the cyclic effect of retaliation breeding revenge from the child, which in turn leads to our retaliating. I use this word—retaliation—on purpose as adults tend to frame our behaviors and responses, especially with children, in nicer and more sophisticated terms. As the adult we need to be candid with ourselves, how we feel, and how we act. Retaliation at its very best can only promote the "Duel-logue."

ASK A QUESTION YOU ALREADY KNOW THE ANSWER TO.

The term I use for this is "trapping."

If you ask Sarah a question that you already know the answer to, you are simply setting her up to lie. When she lies, then you have a whole new issue to deal with, honesty. But ask yourself this, were you being honest asking a question you knew the answer to? It is a fact of life that children lie, "fudge," deny, excuse, evade, etc. and it is their first inclination to do so when confronted by an adult.

If you know what happened and need to confront Sarah on the behavior, say so, "Sarah I need to talk with you about getting in late last night." Rather than setting her up to lie with, "Sarah, were you late last night?" If you can be more specific do so, "Sarah I need to talk with you about being out thirty minutes later than we agreed."

With the first and especially the third statement you are confronting without criticizing or condemning. You have given Sarah a clear message as to what your concern is, enough information so she knows you are not guessing or "fishing" for a response, and a reminder that she did not follow a mutual agreement.

When I first started in this profession, I received two sound pieces of advice, one from the superintendent of the facility and the other from my immediate supervisor.

The superintendent on my very first day simply stated, "Gary, all kids lie. But it usually takes one of us adults to give them the opportunity. Don't set a kid up!" When I asked what he meant he elaborated, "Kids are going to lie if asked a question that affords them the chance. So if you know the answer to the question and you go ahead and ask it, don't get upset if you receive a lie in response, you got what you asked for!"

I then asked this gentleman, how do you handle a situation when you know the child has misbehaved, how do I address the issue? His response was to simply be open and honest and express what you know to be a fact (much in the manner described in the statement to Sarah cited above). He also advised not to believe everything I heard about a child's behavior from others, give the kid a chance and if he is goofing up, I would see it first hand when I could then be sure and my intervention more appropriate.

My immediate supervisor, the first day on the job, handed me a 300 page manual, told me to read it, and as she walked away stated, "Oh yeah, Gary. Whatever you do, don't lie to a kid, he will never forget it, and you can forget being any good for him."

These two people were almost polar opposites in philosophy and work style, to the point I am not sure they could agree on where to eat lunch, even if it was free. However, they were giving me the same message, be honest, be candid, stick to the facts, and don't set kids up for failure. Doing so would afford me the opportunity to have a better chance of hearing the true story and providing some assistance to the child. I have found this to be true, and highly recommend following their sage advice.

GIVE ADULT MOTIVATION AND SOPHISTICATION TO A CHILD'S BEHAVIOR.

Children are children, with the experiences of a child. Although it seems we as a society are rushing them into adulthood, we need to remember they are kids; they do not act due to the same motivations or in the sophisticated manner of adults. If you look at a child and see a littler version of an adult, such as Mini Me, you are missing out on a beautiful experience, and the child is being cheated. It would be like looking at a fantastic rainbow and complaining it is raining!!

Many adults do not seem to grasp this concept, especially in a parental role. I worked with one young man, bright, well educated, good family background, who really wanted to help kids. However, for reasons unknown to me, his perception of children was that they were natural born liars. A child's story, in his opinion, was going to hold more untruths than truths. He read into a child's behavior, especially his errors and misbehavior, adult motivations and sophistication.

Children do not live their lives like a chess master plotting and planning three to four steps ahead in the game. As may be imagined, this young man did not last long in the field as he was unable to build positive relationships with children. Unfortunately, this later spilled over into his own life. I ran into him at the grocery store one day and inquired as to his wife and three year old son. The first words out of his mouth were, "Well, he's like any kid, he already knows how to lie and manipulate!"

My heart went out to that little boy, condemned at age three by his dad as a liar and manipulator. My guess is the boy will become quite good at being dishonest and manipulation. Some of you might think, "Ah ha! Karma!" I don't know about that, but it does seem we get what we set ourselves up for!

CRITICIZE

Human beings, like plants, grow in the soil of acceptance, not in the atmosphere of rejection."
-John Powell

No matter what we might tell ourselves, none of us like to be criticized. Very seldom do we see criticism as a statement about our behavior; we tend to view it as an attack on our persona. This is even truer when we are not very secure in who we are and what we are doing, which is the case with most of the children for whom we provide care. Usually criticism escalates our emotions, tends to assign blame, and raises our defensive postures and responses. Criticizing Sarah puts the focus on her persona and strains your relationship when what she needs and your true desire is for her to look at her behavior.

HOLD A GRUDGE

As adults, we like to think of this as a childish behavior, but most of the people I know who hold on to grudges are in fact adults. Let bygones be bygones. Do not keep harping on the error. If it is repeated by Sarah, treat each occurrence as a single episode and a choice acted upon at that specific time. If you start to see a behavior pattern, it can be pointed out and discussed in a positive manner, minus the nagging reminders. An older gentleman I worked with in child care was good at reminding me that tomorrow is a new day, a new chance for a child to grow, and as the adult; we had to wipe the slate clean. If we kept a record of every transgression, that is all we would have time to do. If we made things worse by reminding the child, he was very apt to provide a repeat performance.

"Discipline is positive. Discipline is training. Teaching and discipline are inseparable".
-Jean Fleming

So what can you do??

THE TO DO LIST...

REMIND YOURSELF TO RELAX AND DEMONSTRATE PATIENCE.

Some of the behavior or misbehavior has a history with the child; it has been going on for some time and obviously meets a need or purpose for Sarah. It may very well have nothing to do with you or her new surroundings. It is not apt to change overnight and will probably take time and incremental steps of change. If you expect a "snap to it" performance from her, you are setting the both of you up for disappointment and failure.

BE REALISTIC IN YOUR EXPECTATIONS.

Ask yourself if your expectations are something the child has the age, maturity, know how, and developmental ability to meet. (In fact, this is probably a good question for every parent to ask themselves on a daily basis.) If not, then adjust those expectations. Our kids do not need more failures.

Years back I had a young man who was twelve, Richie, and he had numerous issues. One of the things I tried to do—with the help of many of our staff—when I came to our agency was to get our residents involved in as many age normal activities, Boy Scouts, pep club, sports as possible. Richie liked playing baseball so we got him set up on a little league team where I knew the coach. When I discussed this with his psychiatrist—a big bear of a man with the spirit and demeanor of a lamb—he reminded me that some sports are not best for kids like Richie. Dr. _____ was very supportive of what we were trying to do but cautioned to get our kids involved in team sports where failure was not so evident, like soccer (unless you were in goal).

Baseball, he wisely pointed out, is a game where your errors are YOUR ERRORS, when you strike out everyone is watching, and most players, even in the majors, only get a hit three out of every ten times. His point was well taken and although Richie finished out the year, doing pretty well, I held on to that advice in the years and residents to come.

As to your family, be realistic in the expectations you place on yourself and your support system.

One of the most unfortunate situations I was a party to involved foster parents who became adoptive parents (the roles seem very similar but there are definite differences). These people had the best of intentions, but way too high expectations and standards for themselves. The adoptive mother held herself to a standard Mother Teresa would have found trying, if not impossible. She also expected her husband to follow suit.

His expectations, however, were a little more grounded but still more than what was healthy and sustainable. Problems truly became significant when they transferred those standards to the children placed in their home who had no ways or means to even come close to their expectations.

All parties in the family appeared to be failing in the relationships required to maintain a "substitute family." This particular family became so stressed it could not function. The children were actually asking the social workers involved to get out. The family, for all intents and purposes, fragmented and all members suffered. The social workers, therapists, and friends all tried to intervene, but the expectations they held were based on the false assumption that, "We are solid enough; we do not need any help." Offers of intervention and support not only fell on deaf ears but turned into resentment leading to further conflicts as the extended family and support system were told to mind their own business.

Who suffered the most? The children, of course. One of their false assumptions which morphed into an expectation was that since they had success with their first foster child, they expected success with every child. It did not, however, transfer to the next two children placed, and from then on it was all downhill, including their relationship with their first child.

When these parents, who were dedicated and hard-working, could not do what they thought they could do, their thinking became distorted. They blamed the "new kids" on not meeting expectations, thus it was "them" not "us," who needed to change behavior.

I would like to report that this was the only family who had such problems, but I cannot. Far too often I have witnessed good and well intentioned people get involved in being a "substitute parent," and struggle due to unrealistic expectations of self and the children in their care.

Please be realistic and know your limitations. Please do the same for the child.

GIVE RESPONSIBILITY FOR THE BEHAVIOR TO THE CHILD.

I have heard a number of child and adolescent experts refer to the "democratic" family, and I have also used this term. Call it what you will, the idea is to have Sarah share with you what she thinks her behavior warrants, the positive as well as the negative. What should be the rewards or consequences, both immediate and long term? When a youngster misbehaves and is approached in this manner it has been my experience that she will be considerably harsher on herself than if the adult had decided the consequence. This gives you the opportunity to demonstrate democratic values of "fairness" and "justice," tempered with a little mercy when she comes down too hard on herself.

By doing so you are demonstrating values that she can learn and utilize, being fair, applying justice, and showing mercy. This also can help her set standards she can use in the future for herself—discipline as well as providing an initiation into the realm of establishing her own boundaries. Giving responsibility for the behavior to Sarah includes her making the necessary amends, restitution, and generally cleaning up her own mess, be it physical, relational, or emotional.

Children who have had traumatic experiences at times tend to be too harsh on themselves, exacting, if allowed, more severe punishment of self than we would enact.

Just the other day I had a young man suspended from school the same week as his Court review and pending discharge. After attempting to rationalize his misbehavior and discussing the situation with me, he traversed the complete spectrum of "complete innocence," to "I hate myself for messing this up," and although seventeen years old was sobbing. After my initial surprise at this comment, I was able, in time, to work through this with him and move him from a sense of self-loathing to the point of self-disappointment.

Kids have trouble making those distinctions without our help. I wanted him to feel disappointed in himself; his behavior warranted such a feeling. I did not want him to "hate" himself. Being disappointed in one self can lead to changing the behavior, making amends, and going on. Self-hatred leads to nothing but negative feelings, thoughts, and subsequently behavior.

At times your efforts may fall short of your hoped for goal. But, you have introduced the concept of self-responsibility to Sarah and at least have a starting point for a real conversation, a "dual-logue" rather than the argumentative "duel-logue."

MORE OF THE "DO'S"

REWARD AND REINFORCE APPROPRIATE BEHAVIOR

Keep your eye on the prize. Remember, your efforts with Sarah and similar children are a journey and neither you nor she will reach the destination easily in giant leaps and bounds. Roadblocks will arise and side roads will be taken, sometimes by choice and sometimes by design. Don't lose sight of what she is doing right, keep the focus on the appropriate behavior she demonstrates and apply the rewards and positive reinforcement.

As you get to know Sarah you will become aware of the things she enjoys, use those as incentives, and engage her in developing her own rewards.

I do not mean to belabor this point, but think in terms of a "kinder, gentler, more positive" Godfather. Whereas Don Corleone would make an offer that could not be refused (unless willing to suffer dire consequences), you want to make an offer that is too enticing not to take. When Sarah gives you the negative behavior, use the incentive and turn the encounter into a positive. Make her an offer she won't refuse. This works very well with younger children but can be utilized with a little ingenuity with children of all ages.

Sarah may love to talk on the phone with her friends or spend time on the internet. At the same time, you need her compliance and cooperation to finish a chore, study for a test, etc. Using the "Godfather" approach you might say something along the lines of, "Hey Sarah, when you get _____ completed let me know, the phone is yours for _____." Using the word WHEN, and being proactive, rather than the word IF, implies that she will get ____ done or not be able to use the phone. IF implies she has no choice in the matter. Realizing, of course, she always has the choice to comply or not to comply, but your message sets the tone for compliance and cooperation, or the reverse.

This approach is similar to the method known as "Grandma's rule." Grandmas, especially my wife, are tremendous at gaining compliance by adding a desired incentive when compliance is met. My wife almost always involves something to do with her being actively involved… playing a game, taking a walk, etc. Kids of all ages like being involved in doing things with the adults with whom they have a good relationship.

My grandma's both used this approach with considerable success. I loved blackberry cobbler, and detested green beans. My grandma would make the cobbler if I picked the berries, but I could not eat the cobbler unless I made an attempt to eat the green beans served at dinner. Of course the incentive was the cobbler, which I had worked for, but had to earn. The "offer I could not refuse" was reinforced by my work, as well as the aroma of warm blackberry cobbler. If I ate the beans rather than just tasting them, there was always a good chance of ice cream served on top of the cobbler, an added bonus. All of us love an unexpected added bonus!

CONSEQUENCES SHOULD "FIT" THE BEHAVIOR.

As we work to instill self-discipline in a child, there will be times when the structure and rules will need the support of consequences for violations and choosing not to behave within the boundaries established.

So what do you do when Sarah breaks a rule or goes outside of a parameter?

The consequence proven to have the biggest impact on anyone, child or adult, is the "natural" consequence. I leave home without an umbrella knowing there is a good chance for rain, it rains, I get wet, I therefore suffer the "natural" consequence of my choice.

Children, too, learn best when they have to deal with the natural consequences of their behavior.

If Sarah chooses to sleep in and is late getting on the school bus, the best consequence is for her to have to walk to school. If she is tardy upon arrival, she has to face the school authorities who have another type of consequence she will have to face, the "logical" consequence.

A "logical" consequence is applied by an external source in lieu of the natural consequence. Usually logical consequences are used when a natural consequence cannot be allowed to take place due to health, safety, and welfare reasons. At times the logical will be used as the natural consequence is of no import to the child, might run counter to the child's best interest at the time, or simply be ignored. Sarah sleeps late, she gets to school late, she misses class and what was taught... the natural consequences are she had to find transportation, and she lost out on the subject matter she missed, neither of which matters to her. To reinforce getting up and being on time for class the logical consequence is applied... you take her to school and charge a transportation fee, she receives detention, misses a school activity, etc.

In my situation, many of our children have school problems—attendance, grades, behavior. We cannot let them be late and suffer natural consequences, so therefore we have to apply "logical" consequences. We transport our residents, but if they are late and we have to make an extra trip, their weekly allowance is "charged" a transportation fee. If the problem becomes persistent, we may up the consequence to loss of a weekend activity or privilege.

In your role as the substitute parent, you might want to allow natural consequences to run their course, but due to the reasons for placement of Sarah and her history and previous experiences, you cannot allow her to suffer the severity of the consequence.

I had a fourteen year old young lady who had major truancy problems at school. She was in the eighth grade and happened to cut class one day and got caught in a downpour. The assistant principal called and told me the story and asked us to bring her a change of clothes. Thinking as to natural consequences, I thought it best if she had to attend the remainder of the day, three classes, damp and uncomfortable (what I would have wanted to do with my kids).

Thankfully, he reminded me of this girl's history. One of her issues was being made fun of at school; therefore he thought it counterproductive for her to remain damp and uncomfortable. He was right, Gary was wrong. Gary took the clothes, talked to the young lady briefly, and thanked the assistant principal for his intervention with me on her behalf! Quite honestly if it had been one of my children, I would have done what my wife told me to do, as she was frequently more on target with them than I was.

It is important that both the logical and applied consequences utilized fit the behavior it is invoked to modify. Engage the child on the specific behavior you want to address and see changed. Refrain from generalization when applying the consequence.

Generalization, in such a case, usually is manifested in nagging or "piling on" behavior by the adult. If you restrict Sarah's phone use for sleeping too late and missing the bus, only restrict for that episode. It is very tempting to add on (pile on) for something of a similar nature that happened recently, which you did not address at the time. "You know, Sarah, you were late the other night, too, so I'm adding two more days of phone restriction." This behavior is seen as being vindictive and "piling on," which makes little if any sense to the child. You may think it is discipline, they see it as punitive.

Such behavior leads the child to focus on the nature of the punishment rather than looking at how she might modify her behavior.

Be careful to choose logical consequences that do not restrict the child from doing something that serves a very positive purpose in her life. I knew a family that was notorious for falling into this pattern. They were very concerned that their thirteen year old son was too reclusive and socially isolated from peers. He finally found an interest in school, after many attempts, which happened to be playing chess. He was pretty good and became involved in the Chess Club, which met two times a week after school.

The parents were almost ecstatic in his new associations. However, when he had a couple of issues about completing homework, the first thing they decided to restrict was his Chess Club involvement, and refused to let him attend a local competition. This was not received very well by their son and he chose to quit the team rather than face accepting their consequences. Who won? No one, in fact both parties lost and harsh feelings and a very cold atmosphere was reported in the family for that particular week.

The youngster refused to return to the Chess Club as he felt it would be taken away with his next misdeed. The same thing happened later with a new interest and this young man withdrew even farther from both his classmates and parents. Utilizing consequences that restrict healthy activity makes no sense. It would be like restricting yourself from the gym and exercise class for having broken your diet by eating ice cream.

I can remember during my seventh grade year being grounded for sixteen weeks. I am unsure what I did to warrant such a restriction, but my math grades were a major factor, as well as my lack of effort. I do remember the punishment and my reaction was "so what." I was smart enough not to say this out loud, but my response in today's world might have been the universal, "Whatever." It did not make a lot of sense to me back then and it did not hit me in an area I truly cared about as I did not go anywhere except outside to play basketball.

Around week fifteen of the "grounding," my parents realized it was not having the desired effect. My math grade was not improving, nor was my effort. My father finally decided to take a drastic measure in his mind, restricting my favorite activity, which was playing basketball. He informed me that he and my mother had decided that if I failed to bring my math book home three nights a week, he would place my ball in the attic for one week. Being a basketball coach, this bothered him but he felt the immediacy might get results. Neither of my parents was concerned as to how they "framed" this message. It was years before the Godfather movie was made, but their concept was similar to Don Corleone's. I had a choice, it was immediate, three nights a week the math book came home or I lost the ball. Now that is not the same as "sleeping with the fishes" per the Don, but the ball was the only one in the neighborhood, thus penalizing my friends.

My father informed me he would not stand over me and make me study but he could see to it that the book was available. I brought it home without fail from that point on, studied very little, but more so than before, with minimal results on my grade. When my dad offered his help, I studied more and my grade did improve.

The "piling on" of the grounding had not worked, but they were able to come up with a means of improving my performance. My parents did not take away the right to go out and play basketball or do what I wanted, but my ball was in quarantine. They did not nag or remind me of their decision and it was my choice to comply or not. I knew from past experience that once they made their decision it was not subject to reconsideration or negotiation.

CONSISTENCY

I believe it was Mark Twain who said that the only truly consistent people to be found in the world are to be located in graveyards.

Children like Sarah have experienced very little consistency from most adults in her life. You need to stand firm and committed on your values and the few important rules, the ELEPHANTS, of your home. Children are masters at splitting and applying pressure on you or your partner to bend if not break. You need, she needs, consistency by you in the parental role.

There will be an occasion or two when you cannot remain consistent. You may choose to change a decision or rule, grant clemency, and show mercy when it is needed and called for more so than enforcement. You may decide a "different" approach is in order to shake things up a little.

It is like being an effective baseball pitcher. A good pitcher does not throw strike after strike unless he wants to see the ball hit over the fence time after time. He will mix up his pitches, throwing a curve when the hitter expects a fastball, thus keeping the hitter on his toes and guessing.

You can do this by simply offering "hurdle help" rather than demanding compliance. It can be responding with the unexpected as Sarah has become accustomed to the norm. You cross her up with a "new pitch" to see if this generates a little progress or at least causes her to stop and reconsider.

When you do enforce the rule and deliver the "bad news" to Sarah, be sure you connect with her. Remember your body language, eye contact, facial expression, and tone of voice all need to be congruent with your message. Be direct, don't assume, nor be vague or flippant with your choice of words. Ask for feedback as to what she heard you say.

It is very interesting when I have such a discussion with a youngster how many times he did not "get" the message I thought I had "sent." I usually ask the child, "Tell me what you think it is I just said?" I get the response, correct it if necessary, then ask, "You don't have to agree with me, but do you understand what was meant and how this affects you?"

After this response, I then state, "How do you feel about this, what do you think?"

These questions tend to get the child engaged in the process and open up room for discussion or at least clarification. In family therapy sessions I often ask these questions to the child after a statement by the parent. At times the parent is amazed as to the actual message their child received as opposed to the message they thought they had sent.

If you are considering the need to establish a new rule, schedule, or consequence, get the child's input and feedback prior to initiating the rule or applying the consequence. No one likes getting blindsided and Sarah's input might be of significant assistance and importance. It is easier to modify and alter a rule or consequence not yet in effect rather than to change such after it is in place.

CONSTRUCTIVE ENGAGEMENT

On the "do not do" list was the use of criticism. When you are direct, open, honest, and connected to the child, you are utilizing "constructive engagement," which is almost the direct opposite of criticism.

Construction is related to building. Constructive engagement is a partnership offer to Sarah to discuss the problem at hand with mutual respect. It promotes solutions, avoids ridicule or personal attacks, and provides support. Utilizing constructive engagement helps Sarah break down the behavior or issue into increments that she can understand and, with concrete help, be improved. It also offers skills to correct and behavioral steps to avoid the problem or issue, as well as an opportunity for Sarah to give feedback and participate in resolution.

Feedback should be handled much the same way as questions you know the answer to; don't ask for feedback unless you are willing to hear it with an open mind. If you respond to Sarah's misbehavior is a situation that requires a definite restriction or penalty, feedback and a subsequent debate serves no positive purpose. This does not mean Sarah cannot have her time to voice her opinion, which should almost always be a part of the process as it can be a major de-escalator.

An example of criticism as opposed to constructive engagement:

Sarah: "I'm leaving, see you around 10 PM."

Parent: "Don't be late like last week, no booze or drugs with your weirdo friends!"

Parent who engages:

Parent: "OK, Sarah, have a good time, remember I need you home by 10 PM sharp. No exceptions tonight, please. Call me if you need a ride or anything, I'll be up."

Another example:

Parent, upon entering a messy kitchen after Sarah made a snack: "Who made this mess? Get in here and clean it now!"

Parent who engages: "Sarah as soon as you are done with your snack I need you to clean up the kitchen area, I have to start dinner soon."

"I" STATEMENTS

A skill to be honed and turned into a habit when using constructive engagement is the use of "I" statements. These are direct and a clear statement of what it is you expect and want with a reason for compliance. "I" statements are specific and objective, avoiding the tendency to generalize or blame, and framed in a non-threatening manner. A format for an "I" statement is as follows:

"When you _____ (the behavior exhibited of concern) I feel _____ (state your feeling) due to/because _____ (a clear statement of the effect the behavior has on you, her, the family, etc.).

Using one of the above examples to demonstrate an "I" statement;

"Sarah, when you don't clean up after you use the kitchen, I get irritated because it leaves me extra work before cooking dinner."

Be concrete and specific as to her behavior that is the problem or concern. If you don't, Sarah may interpret the situation as you not wanting her to eat a snack, using the kitchen, and running up the food bill. Don't give her reason to misconstrue your concern and the message delivered.

When you reveal how you feel, strive for accuracy and don't exaggerate. Using another scenario from the above...

Parent: "Sarah when you are late I get worried you might be hurt or in an unsafe situation."

Be as concrete and specific as possible as to the effects of Sarah's behavior, on her, you, and the family. She is more apt to change her behavior if she has a clear picture as to the effects of such on everyone involved.

Utilizing "I" statements and constructive engagement are not skills that are easily mastered as it is a different way of talking for most adults and parents. Old habits are difficult to break, but the children we parent need us to do so. More often than not, they will not respond to our old tried and true ways.

During a family counseling session with one family, I was attempting to get the mother to utilize "I" statements with her fourteen year old son. George had been in a number of placements and foster homes over the last couple of years, due mainly to conflicts with his mother in their home. What started as minor disagreements escalated into full blown physical altercations, leading to George's removal from the home. It was my task to work with his mother and George to "transition" him home over a three month period.

In the course of our sessions, I introduced them to the concept of "I" statements and how to utilize them. George had told me he always felt like he was under a verbal attack from his mother the moment he walked into the house. Issues might be homework, house chores, whatever. She had something negative and hostile to say most afternoons during their first encounter. He would either react with hostility or leave the home. As we discussed the concept and skill, practicing with familiar scenarios from their home, it was obvious George's mother had doubts and was skeptical of this skill... she was a tough student to say the least. At the end of a particularly trying session, she turned to George and stated, "I don't know about you George, but these "I" statements seem like a pile of shit to me."

After a very long hour of work, this was not what I wanted to hear. However, I chose to respond with an "I" statement, in effect, asking her if the work we were doing was as "shitty" as having her son sent away from her home. She agreed it was not and that maybe the work and new skills might help in their relationship.

I did note her honesty in the session and it served to open up room for discussion, as well as pointing out the need for realistic practice.

MODEL THE BEHAVIOR YOU WANT TO SEE.

Instilling self-discipline and discipline in a child's life who has had very little of either will take you being in the active lead as the "Role Model."

Appropriate role models for children in today's society are extremely difficult to find and even more difficult to get the child to model the behavior. Celebrity, status, notoriety, fame, and wealth are all characteristics that are enticing to a child. Those who possess such, the "rich and famous," as well as the notorious so to speak, are familiar names to children and often who they choose to emulate. Think of those you know who are constantly in the spotlights of the media... how many would you hold up as good examples of discipline and self-discipline? My guess is very few.

Sarah has not been exposed to adults who consistently behave in a disciplined or self-disciplined manner. You cannot expect her to exert self-discipline if you do not demonstrate both every single day, episode after episode, with all you are in contact with.

Your relationship with Sarah will be the most important factor you bring to any encounter with her. What kind of role model you are will have the most impact on that relationship.

So, what is expected from a parental role model? Some of the aspects have been covered elsewhere in this book, but it is very important to be...

Present

Respectful

Honest

Dependable

Trustworthy   .

Predictable

Sarah needs to know you are there, physically present and in tune to her needs. She is not used to this attention and it may be perceived, initially, as your being a "busybody," "nosey," or "watch dog." Those early perceptions may cause a few upheavals, but hang in there; you staying the course and riding out her emotional thunderstorms will pay dividends.

She needs to know that what you said yesterday remains the same today. You don't change your behavior, rules, routines, and expectations without very good reason and then you give ample notice to all involved.

When you goof up, admit it, apologize, and point out your human foibles. Do not set yourself up as some perfect specimen of what God had in mind when he thought of parents!

Don't expect or ask for thanks or appreciation. When the thanks come, they will be more genuine and have a deeper meaning for you and Sarah.

"The greatest way to live with honor in this world, is to be what we pretend to be."
-Socrates

MAKE THE COMMITMENT... KEEP THE COMMITMENT

Commitment is essential to your role as a substitute parent. Sarah might be in your home one week, one year, or the remainder of her childhood and adolescence. Approach her stay as if it will be for a lifetime. So many children have had too many adults "cut and run" in their lives. Sarah expects this behavior from adults, including you. She expects you will give up or give in when tested, and she is a veteran at both testing adults and watching then head for the hills. Telling her you are committed means very little. Showing her you are committed means everything. A line from a novel I read has always stuck in my mind and says it all... *SINCERITY WITHOUT ACTION IS BULLSHIT!*

Or as John Mellencamp wrote in his song *Perfect World...*

"These are just words, and words are OK. It's what you do not what you say. If you're not part of the future then get out of the way."

Children, in particular adolescents, have great B.S. detectors when it comes to adults. Unfortunately these same detectors go on the blink when it comes to their peers! Your words will be suspect unless backed up by your behavior. Your actions will always speak louder than anything you say.

Sarah may not remember all the times you have kept your commitment to her, but I guarantee that one lie, one broken promise, one failure to keep a commitment will not be so easily forgotten, and may erode all that you have worked so hard to establish. It is as if you have pushed Humpty Dumpty off the wall again.

"Making commitments generates hope. Keeping commitments generates trust."
-Blaine Lee

This is not to say you cannot and will not make mistakes and errors. It happens to the best of parents in the best of situations. Don't beat yourself up for honest errors. An honest effort, even if it is wrong or does not work, can still be appreciated by a child and have a positive impact.

During my interviews with potential residential child care workers, I always asked a question or two about the applicant's athletic background. Did you play, coach, manage, etc? If so I would then use the analogy of the shortstop in baseball. Generally the shortstop is the best athlete on the field, quick on his feet, and quick thinking. Shortstop gets a lot of action, the ball is hit, and he reacts. I would then advise the applicant that I wanted a "shortstop" child care worker. Someone who was quick on his feet and who would try to make every play possible. I did not care if errors were committed, that comes with the position while trying to make the right play. The errors I could not tolerate were errors of omission, not going after the ball, giving up on the play, dogging it.

The same is true in your role as the substitute parent. Errors of omission with a child will destroy any chance of building a relationship. Errors of commission, when you were giving it your all, can not only be understood but also forgiven and forgotten.

When we mess up and make a mistake, it is best simply to fess up and admit the error. After all we know it, the child knows it, so no one is going to be fooled when we don't step up and admit our goof ups.

Being honest about our own behavior, both the positive and not so positive, also serves as a model to the child in our care.

"The man who makes no mistakes does not usually make anything."
-William Connor Magee

Apologizing to a child can be a very significant and poignant event for the child.

I have made my fair share of mistakes over the years that have necessitated apologizing to the youngster involved. One such encounter that has stayed in my mind was with a young man named Steve. I was the administrator at the time and erred first by jumping to a conclusion, then compounded that error by public admonishment of Steve (another error) for what I thought was his misbehavior.

When I realized all of my errors, I felt a public apology was necessary as it was a public admonishment. I also wanted to model this behavior for the other staff members as well as residents. At dinner, prior to prayer,

I asked for everyone's attention and proceeded to apologize, admitting both errors. I stated that even if my conclusion had been correct, I had no right to address this in a public manner. I expressed my regrets to Steve and returned to my office while dinner commenced.

Very shortly thereafter, Steve was standing in my office door and was visibly upset, with tears in his eyes. When I inquired as to what was bothering him he replied, "Gary, that was the first time in my life a grown up apologized to me. Why did you do that, you didn't have to?" I told Steve I had erred and felt it is important to acknowledge such regardless of my age or position, or for that matter his. I advised him I knew better and should have acted in a more mature and responsible manner.

Steve did accept the apology but, as he walked out of my office, he requested that I never apologize to him in public; he did not know how to handle it. I apologized for that and we both started laughing.

This young man, by the way, had been sexually molested for a couple of years by various boyfriends of his mother. None of those people were ever held accountable nor did they apologize to him. In later conversations I learned that Steve's mother had neither acknowledged the abuse nor had she apologized for his treatment.

"An apology is a lovely perfume; it can transform the clumsiest moment into a gracious gift."
-Margaret Runbeck

Chapter 9

How do I accommodate Johnny's "taste" in friends, music, clothes?

"Just living in not enough," said the butterfly, "one must have sunshine, freedom, and a little flower."
-Hans Christian Anderson

You can absolutely bet your bottom dollar that there will be distinct and major differences in your views and Johnny's when it comes to dress, music, and friends.

You may never come to totally accept his "tastes" nor can you expect him to adopt yours as his.

How you choose to handle those issues will determine if you can find some common grounds, accommodations, tolerance, and build bridges rather than erect barriers.

I had the privilege of licensing and working with a very dynamic young couple as foster parents a few years back. This couple had one small child of their own and was willing to accept a child with multiple problems who I had removed from his parents care. This particular couple was strongly influenced by their faith to provide foster care, and were devout practitioners. Providing care was not only their way of helping a child but it was also fulfillment of their religious calling. They had a saying in their home that they were very up front with, "Garbage in, means garbage out." Their argument was if you allow questionable or detrimental things into your home, you were going to have to deal with the ramifications. Obviously they had strict guidelines on television, reading and entertainment material, for anyone in their home. They did quite well working with younger children but realized they were not going to be successful with adolescents who had already developed their own "tastes" in such matters.

I did not disagree with their statement, then or now.

However, as "substitute parents," you will need to give considerable thought to your standards and how those might impact a child placed in your home. What are the standards you view as absolutes... no flex/no bend, and what are the issues you can be more flexible and allow time for acclimation.

Acclimation time, especially for adolescents, is very important. If you can "grin and bear it," or occasionally "grimace and bear it," in regards to the more superficial issues, I think you will have a better chance at success.

"Every child has a right to its own bent… It has a right to find its own way and go its own way, whether that way seems wise or foolish to others."
-George Bernard Shaw

One of those issues is appearance. Johnny may come to your home looking as if he has slept in a trash bin for weeks, and he may have. Give it a little time. What he is wearing might not be of his choice. It may well be the only things he has from his former home and family and have considerable emotional value as a part of his identity.

Sam came into our facility as a rail thin, hunched over, fourteen year old with his hair hanging in his eyes, and a generally "droopy" appearance. We were aware he had a history of excessive use of marijuana, daily, and a reputation (his identity) as a "stoner." He wore a dirty old fatigue jacket handed down by male members in his family since Vietnam. This jacket was vital to his identity and a real connection to his family.

It was important, if we were going to connect with Sam, that we leave the jacket issue alone, except to offer professional cleaning. We focused on getting him involved in other activities that did not involve the use of marijuana and over time, within a month or two, his total appearance changed. The hair was cut, by his choice, his posture improved, he looked you in the eye, and he started to fill out from decent food and exercise. It took a few more months for him to outgrow the jacket, literally and figuratively, but we kept it as a keepsake. He left placement a year later, in foster care with the jacket packed.

I use this only as an example of focusing on the important key issues and letting some of the superficial slide. It is amazing as Sam developed relationships and got involved in other activities how the importance of appearing as a "stoner" diminished. He adopted a new persona, to the point that when he left we got out his admission picture and all had a good laugh. He recalled his first day and the care we took with the jacket as making him feel welcomed and not putting him down. He admitted coming into the program angry and ready to fight on all issues, but instead of meeting a combative staff he met a cooperative and empathetic group of adults willing to let him adjust.

When I think of appearance and such superficial issues, I am reminded of my Grandmother Meyer. She came to my rescue after one particularly "testy" family get together when my haircut (or lack of one) as well as my clothing were the topics of some criticism. When I took her home that night she turned to me and said, "Gary, I am not worried about what is on top of your head, it is more important as to what is in your head." She then tapped me on my chest where my fringe jacket hung and said," I don't care what covers your heart; I care what is in your heart." I have never forgotten that encounter and have used similar words many times over the years to convey the same message.

"I implore you to see with a child's eyes, hear with a child's ears, and to feel with a child's heart."
-Dr. Antonio Novello

If you get caught up in who the child seems to be (Sam the droopy stoner), you will never know who he really is or wants to be. Treat the child as you want him to be and lo and behold, you might start seeing that person evolve in front of your eyes.

This takes patience and tolerance and time. Look for incremental changes and again apply positive reinforcement. When Sam started filling out and outgrowing his jacket, we offered to take him shopping for something new, not to replace the old, but to meet the new needs of his physical stature. Had we offered to do so his first week or month before he saw and felt the need, we would have been in a power struggle we could not have won.

As to music, reading material, video games, etc., the above applies. Obviously you must set your standards. But flex where you can. For example, I did not care for my son's taste in music during his high school years... gangster rap (or what I thought was gangster rap) which demeaned women and extolled the virtues of drugs and violence. That is what I heard, he heard something entirely different and until we spoke about it I could not see his point of view (my father did not care for the Rolling Stones in the 60's, my favorite group, for the same reasons). I would have preferred he adopt different musical tastes… fat chance, especially with my stated opposition. It was agreed he could listen as long as his sister, mother, and I could not hear it.

His interest in Tupac Shakur led to our talking about Tupac's mother who was a former Black Panther militant. This conversation segued into many discussions regarding the 1960s, civil rights, the influence of music on politics, Bob Dylan, how people progress and evolve, on and on and those discussions continue today. His interest was piqued in those topics and I became a little more knowledgeable and understanding of the influence and importance of rap and such artists as Tupac.

As to the reading material, I am pretty happy if a child reads, period. Unless it is pornography, I choose not to get upset about what a child reads. Again provide healthy alternatives. If a child is reading too much fantasy comics, introduce him to other types of fiction that come close to his taste. Share some of the reading material, and as much as it might pain you to read what he is reading, to do so opens up new paths to communication. If he is hooked on "superheroes," introduce him to some real heroes, over time, who did similar things he admires from his "superhero."

This holds true for movies and DVDs. Start where the child is and broaden those horizons as mentioned with reading. It is important to point out, when the opportunity presents, what is really "real" and what is fake. It is important to get his idea on those subjects first. Again not to pick on my son, but one snowy winter break he and a good friend got involved playing a video game, pretty graphic in nature, involving shooting an enemy foe and advancing levels as you "wasted" the opposition. It concerned me as I am not a fan of this type of entertainment. However, when I talked with both boys they quickly assured me they knew reality from fantasy and it was a one day diversion, but I had to as the parent ask those questions.

I thought I knew they were only playing a "game," but I had to let them know I was monitoring what they were doing and would continue to do so. It was not a heavy handed message of "I don't like this crap!" (although I did not like this crap). I was able to get that message conveyed without it seeming as if I was attacking their taste or idea of fun. I am sure in their minds I was "out of mine." Regardless, kids will listen to your concern if it is your concern and not a confrontation or criticism of them.

Peers, as we should all remember, are extremely important to children, especially adolescents.

Johnny may come into your family with a peer group that gives you concerns or questions. No parent I have ever known has approved 100% with the choices of friends or romantic friends of their children.

The best possible course of action is to open your home to Johnny's friends and encourage activities there or in public places such as school, church, and community recreation areas. The more he is in your home with his friends, the more you will gain in knowledge about him and his choices. He will not change friends based upon your edicts, he will simply change locale as to where he meets and interacts. The interactions are best supervised, monitored, and influenced within your home. Guaranteed there will be one or two people you will wish he did not associate with—provide more structure and follow up with those "suspects." Gather a little more information when he goes out with them or wants to do something that involves those friends. Make your home a haven for safe activity with a few established rules of behavior, and stick by them.

Know who Johnny is hanging out with and get to know their families as much as possible without being a private detective. As Johnny demonstrates good choices, over time you can ease up on some of the restrictions of his activity and freedom.

As to Johnny's friends, don't be too quick to judge. With adolescents all is not what it at first seems to be. Get to know the person before you make rash judgments.

The best way to get to know Johnny's friends, especially the ones you feel are most suspect, is to have them in your home and structure the interaction. It has been my experience the very few who are truly suspect soon tire of the environment being structured and go elsewhere for companionship (this is especially true if it is a romantic involvement/relationship). Your providing structure "crowds" them out and the environment does not afford for them to act in a way you do not approve.

This also allows Johnny to see for himself what his friend is all about. He also sees your accommodation of a person you are unsure of.

"Every sinner has a future, every saint had a past."
-Anonymous

Prepare yourself for introduction to a different language or "lingo." Adolescents in particular use language we are not always "hip to." Likewise, a lot of our language has no meaning to a child today. I have received a number of blank stares from a youngster when I have used such terminology as "he bought the farm" or, "man you are making a tough row to hoe for yourself," just to name a couple. Those young people have no idea what those phrases mean, and they use phrases just as foreign to me.

I do not try to talk like a teen, but I do want to understand what it is they are trying to say. I also catch myself, more and more, asking for clarification, "Hey, this is what I think I heard you say, now what did you mean?" When I talk I very often stop and ask, "Did you hear what I said? I do not need you to agree, but I do need you to understand?"

This can be extremely important at the beginning of a relationship or when you are engaged with a child who does not share your culture or background. I briefly worked with an African American teen whose father I had known years before. Due to my relationship with his dad, he felt more comfortable with me than I actually felt with him. He therefore felt more comfortable using language with me that reflected this association and I needed a lot of clarification. A term of derision towards one person might be taken as a term or respect towards another. In this case he used a term I had heard as derogatory (not the N word) in past experiences, but he meant it with respect in our relationship. Until I voiced my concern and asked for clarification, our initial conversations were not productive.

I also emphasize with any child I work with that the "setting" that is the time and especially the place are important factors in how we choose to communicate.

My standard is a young person can say anything he chooses to me in private. I want to engage him in conversation and if in private how he says what he needs to say is not as important to me as providing him the opportunity to say it. Profanity does not draw my ire if in private. If in public, then I have to respond accordingly as public profanity towards me or others can be misconstrued by other people. The same goes for respect issues... I can tolerate a whole lot more if in the privacy of a one on one discussion or encounter.

We as the adults need to set these parameters. The vast majority of the young people we work with have not had such parameters set or enforced.

When we talk with a young person we want to pay attention to the feeling expressed, not the content or choice of words. If we don't respond to the feeling and focus on the words used, we severely limit the dialogue and get caught in the "duel-logue."

A child may say something very profound, and we can hear it if we choose to not take offense at the profanity it comes wrapped in.

Parents as well as "substitute parents" have asked how do they set rules for the child for when they are not at home, school, and church,

I first of all propose a semantics change going from the word "rules" to "parameters." Rules are made to be broken, parameters are set to provide safety but allow room for movement and growth (much like a fenced in pasture compared to a horse stall, both serve its purpose, but the purpose is different based on the needs of the horse).

Parameters are limits we need to learn to set for ourselves, as does a child, whereas rules are imposed, usually from on high. Children will resent such impositions, whether in their best interest or not. A rule will be viewed as a restriction of freedom and choice, whereas a parameter allows some freedom of movement and choices within a safe limited area.

Think of a bridge crossing a river. A rule is the speed limit, it is for our safety, the guardrails are parameters, for our safety, but allow us some movement from lane to lane and a little buffer space if we veer one way or the other. Your rules should be like a speed limit, safety and health related with a price to pay if exceeded.

However, there are many ways to use parameters when a rule is not needed. Parameters will also allow a child not to go as far as they might dare (self-discipline) rather than a rule they may choose to break or ignore. When we help a child set parameters, we are offering the opportunity for the child to be involved in setting limits and engaging in self-control and self-discipline. Granted this is "wordsmithing" on my part to a degree. But remember the perception of the words by the child is important and can lead to his buy in. How you say something, the terminology utilized, may be as important as what it is you actually said.

What will Johnny respond best to... a parameter that denotes he has control, "Johnny here are the limits and boundaries," or a rule, "Johnny here is the law."

Enough of this... here are the parameters I recommend when it comes to Johnny spending time away from home with friends, on a date, whatever. I call them...

THE FIVE W'S

Who are you going to be with?

What are your plans, what will you be doing?

Where will you be going?

When can I expect you to return?

and if the conversation gets this far...

Why do you want to go?

If the answers to the 5W's are reasonable, then I would recommend giving your consent to the request. If modification is needed, start first with the issues you agree on, then go on to those that need some "tweaking."

One other parameter to throw into the mix is **CHANGE**. With young people very little is concrete when planning events, things constantly change, times, places, people involved. Be sure to indicate that any significant change in one or more of the 5 W's needs to be called back to you. Hopefully you have done the same when the reverse is true; when your plans changed that affected Johnny you called and notified him.

You can discuss what changes you feel are significant and need reporting. Let Johnny know from the start that changes he reports may lead to changes you request in his activity or schedule.

Indicate your willingness and desire to provide **SUPPORT**.

Johnny needs to know you will "cover his back," if he gets into a situation he cannot handle or is heading into trouble. If something goes wrong or feels wrong, he needs to know he can call you and you will come to his assistance or rescue. If he needs you to be the "pain in the butt meddling parent," you can play that role (it comes natural to most of us parents) and bail him out and allow him to save face with his peers. If it is a situation he simply wants out of or not to get into, you will come and pick him up and not say anything at that time. Johnny needs to trust that no matter what, you will respond and the issue, problem or situation can be discussed later. The message being conveyed is, "Johnny, your safety and welfare are of paramount importance to us, you can trust us to support you."

So what do we do if the 5 W's don't get the response you as a parent need?

Think about collaboration, rather than compromise.

Think about getting interests met, rather than positions.

Think about needs, rather than wants (Johnny's and yours).

"Let's you and I conjure together. You watch me and I'll watch you and I will show you how to show me how to show you how to do marvelous human tricks together."
-Courtney Milne

An example might serve to clarify.

Janie, a 12 year old young lady, comes home after school on a Friday and makes the request, "Can I go to the movie tonight with my friend Sally and spend the night at her house?" A reasonable request, with most of the 5 W's answered in her request. However, you know she has her first dance recital, a recital she has worked hard to prepare for and is of importance to her.

Your response is to say no as she needs her rest and you realize she will get little sleep at Sally's.

Janie's position is she wants to go. Your position is she needs to stay home.

Now look at it as a question of interests, not positions.

What is her interest in going to the movie and spending the night at Sally's? You might simply ask her that question, "Janie, what is your interest in going to the movies and spending the night at Sally's?" Her answer may surprise you, it may be she simply wants to see the movie Sally is going to that night, or she may just want to spend some time with a friend.

Once you explore her interest you may find a solution that is mutually satisfying, not a 50 – 50 compromise, which usually leaves both parties 50% satisfied but 50% dissatisfied.

As you ascertain Janie's interest you can indicate yours, you want her rested and fresh for the recital which she wants to perform at her best.

So now you know each other's interest… Janie's is to spend time with a friend, yours is for her to be rested and at her best in the morning.

The next question to pose is, "How might we get both interests met?" Or so that she understands, "OK, Janie how might we both win?" or "How might we get what we need although we might not totally get what we want?"

"What people need and what people want may be very different."
-Elbert Hubbard

This is the key to collaboration, getting both parties interest met.

Both of you can propose possible solutions; the only stipulation is the solution must meet both interests. You, as the adult, may have to help in this process by stating a possible solution. One could be going to the movie with her friend but coming home at a reasonable time so she can go to sleep. You may have to provide transportation to and from the movie. Another solution may be a postponement until the next day following the recital, or a partial postponement of both requests. During this discussion you can bring up ideas and be sure to listen to hers. If you can step back and look at various proposals, it makes it much easier and less confrontational to come up with a mutual decision.

"The reward of a successful collaboration is a thing that cannot be produced by either parties working alone."
-Harlan Ellison

In Janie's case, once each party looked at interest rather than positions, it became apparent they were closer in interest than first thought. Having been a party to this collaborative effort, the results were that Janie stayed home that night. The next day the parent took Janie and her friend, following the recital, to the movie, then back to her home for pizza. The parent had Janie home on Friday night, rested and ready to perform on Saturday morning. Janie got to see the movie with her friend, as well as a couple of others who also could not attend the night before, and actually spent more time with her friends with the pizza party. A "win/ win" situation or solution.

What happens if both parties stick to positions? Think about it, we have all been there with our children. As adults and the authority we usually invoke that authority and make our position stick, "because I said so!" Anytime you hear yourself saying that phrase, take a brief time out and reconsider what you just said, was it necessary, and if so, how might you say this in a more positive manner.

Sticking to positions rather than considering interests has a tendency to lead to harsh words, hurt feelings, no one being satisfied, and both parties feeling upset or at the least cheated.

Dr. Seuss wrote a neat little story about two characters "sticking to their positions," called The Zax. I include it for your consideration and would suggest you watch the video of this sometime with your young person. I have used it at our facility to demonstrate the absurdity of positions versus interests, and collaboration versus stubbornness.

THE ZAX BY DR. SEUSS

The day before today making tracks in the Prairie of the Prax, came a North Going Zax and a South Going Zax. And it happened that both of them came to a place where they bumped.

There they stood Foot to Foot, Face to Face.

"Look here now," the North Going Zax said, "I say you are blocking my path. You are right in my way. I'm a North Going Zax and I always go north. Get out of my way, now and let me go forth."

"Who's in whose way," snapped the South Going Zax, "I always go South, making south going tracks. So you're in my way! And I ask you to move and let me go South in my south going groove."

Then the North Going Zax puffed his chest up with pride, "I never," he said, "take a step to one side. And I will prove it to you that I won't change my ways If I have to keep standing here 59 days!"

"And I'll prove to you," yelled the South Going Zax, "That I can stand here in the Prairie of Praz for 59 years! For I live by a rule that I learned as a boy in South Going School. Never budge! That's my rule. Never budge in the least! Not an inch to the West! Not an inch to the East! I can and I will if it makes you and me and the whole world stand still."

Well of course the world didn't stand still. The world grew. In a couple of years, the new highway came through and they built it right over those two Stubborn Zax. And left them there, standing un-budged in their tracks.

-*The Sneetches and Other Stories,* Dr. Seuss, 2003 Harper Collins Publishers

When the focus is on interests, communication is opened up, and other possibilities for success can be "conjured together," setting a framework for future concerns and collaborative efforts.

This is not always easy to do, but as the adult we need to take the lead.

"It is precisely when we want to give up on collaboration that we most need to return to dialogue, try to listen and open our own way of thinking to new strategies."
-Alicia Rouverol

Chapter 10
How do I deal with Sarah's "real" family?

"The butterfly's attractiveness derives not only from colors, deeper motives contribute to it." -Primo Levi

How do I "work" with Sarah's family?

It had been a very busy difficult holiday period with lots of snow that we folks in southern Indiana are just not used to having to handle.

After four very rough days we were able to get most of the residents off campus for their Christmas visits. I was transporting the last three to leave, dodging the other sliding cars and winding my way across town utilizing side streets.

Trudy, age 18, was my final "drop off" for the day and I, as well as other staff, were used to transporting her as her parents were extremely unreliable. Trudy was in placement with us for the third time since she was thirteen years old and on the brink of leaving the program for an independent living situation.

Her parents were chronic drug users who, when sober, were interested and concerned parents, but unfortunately their sobriety was usually of short duration. Of late they had made significant progress in many areas and Trudy was looking forward to visitation. Trudy and I were discussing their ups and downs while driving across town with the conversation initiated by her. Over the years we had talked about a lot of things, including her parents, and often she was skeptical of their interest and love for her. She could be very negative about them as people in general and particularly parents (two of her siblings were currently in the care of the juvenile authorities and out of town).

When Trudy would open up I utilized active listening and reflective responses, both to encourage her to express her feelings without judgment by me on her or her parents. I deliberately stayed away from endorsing her negative feelings and statements as she was often escalated when being negative and did not need me to inflame those feelings. It was interesting that day as she talked about how we had "talked" and she viewed my comments and lack of comments as being a sign of respect for her parents and her. Trudy was very appreciative of this and prior to leaving the vehicle that day stopped, turned, looked me in the eye, and said, "Thanks for never disrespecting my mom." When I asked why she had thanked me, as Trudy was not known for thanking anyone for anything, she replied, "No matter how angry I got with her, and no matter how many times she has disappointed me, you never said a bad thing about her."

I was astonished at this comment and my first thought was to open my mouth, stick out my tongue, and show her all of the bite marks deriving from our conversations about her family. However, I helped her carry in her belongings and wished her and her folks a Merry Christmas.

As I drove back across town I thought about Trudy, her family, her history, and her comment. All I had truly done was listen, honor her feelings, attempt to reflect her feelings, avoid taking ownership of those feelings, and tried to deescalate her feelings when they boiled over or were too far from the reality of the situation. She saw this as respect for her mother.

Trudy's perception of how I treated her parents was of primary importance to her, more so than how they treated her. This can and will probably be true in your interactions with those children in your care.

Over the years I have had numerous conversations with children who have "failed" in other placements. Some of these children have gone into foster homes and not met with success, resulting in multiple placements. Others have left residential care such as our facility, only to return shortly thereafter as they could not "adjust" to their new family. Some involved in divorces have bounced back and forth from one parent to the other, often with step parents in the mix, never truly settling down in one home or family. I have seen the same with children in relative care going from this aunt to that uncle then back to mom and on to grandma, with similar results.

During these discussions with the various children a few of the major reasons given for not being comfortable and successful are as follows:

"I was treated like a stranger."

"I couldn't be myself."

"I didn't fit in" to the family, neighborhood, school, etc.

"I couldn't see my friends."

"I couldn't handle the rules." (Surprisingly a large number of these children who returned to our facility from foster or relative care report their big issue was the lack of rules and structure they had become accustomed to in placement!)

"Their expectations were too high."

"I didn't get along with their kids," (step dad, step mom, stepsiblings).

However, the three major reasons most often expressed are all related to the child's biological family dynamics.

1) "My parents did not like my (foster parent/step parent/relative)."

2) "I can't call someone else Mom and Dad. They aren't my real family."

3) "They did not respect my real Mom/Dad/Family."

I realize there are other reasons placements fail and children get disrupted and moved more than they should. But we need to pay attention to what the children say and the above is what I heard expressed time after time, with little change in thirty plus years.

So many of the above are directly related to Sarah's feelings of loyalty to her biological or real family as well as her recollection of her life prior to placement, divorce, death, or whatever led to separation.

In the role of the "substitute" parent you need to be cognizant of these feelings and the behavior such might generate.

Accommodation... it is the key, and it is in your hands.

It is your obligation and responsibility to make the necessary accommodations for the benefit of Sarah in regards to her "real" family. Sarah is the individual of prime importance and you are going to have to take the lead and, at least initially, carry the major part of the responsibility.

Sarah and her real family have suffered the loss and their initial thoughts will seldom be on how to accommodate the "new" family. It is unlikely she or they will see it as their obligation to make the best out of what they perceive to be a bad and unfair situation.

Sarah's family will probably feel that they have been treated unjustly, punished, and cut off from Sarah. She may harbor the same feelings and perceptions. This can be just as true in step parent situations, divorces, and relative placements where there is usually at least one aggrieved party. The "real" family, Dad, Mom, can often present as hostile, uncaring, indignant, removed, petty, immature, thoughtless, indifferent, and neglectful.

They feel as if they are being judged, rated, criticized, marginalized, scrutinized, and held to different standards than the substitute parent. Often guilt is a burden they carry or feel over the situation, including cases of divorce, and their loss of Sarah from their lives. They worry that she will either miss them too much, or maybe not miss them enough.

Helplessness can be a pervasive reaction when a child leaves home under such circumstances, and it is magnified if the child has made the choice to leave. Inadequacy issues abound as someone has decided that they are unfit as parents, again this is magnified if that someone is the child. It is easy for the parents to transfer blame to authorities, the "system," Courts, custodial parent, relative, substitute parents, and unfortunately in some cases, the child herself.

When working with the real family members I address these feelings, whether they are evident or not, as soon as the opportunity presents itself. I want the parents to realize they are not that unusual or different from most parents who lose a child. Those feelings are common. However, I emphasize that the child is the priority and what is most important is how they as parents express and deal with those feelings, especially in the presence of the child. I have had many parents voice the concern that they cannot compete—with us, foster home, other parent, stepparent, etc.—especially if the other caregiver offers more material advantages. After acknowledgement of this feeling, I respond that their child will want her own parents regardless, if they meet her needs for **love, recognition, belonging, acceptance, discipline, respect**, and the very basics of material well-being.

If the parents can provide the first six items mentioned above I have yet to have a child refuse to go home based on material advantages or disadvantages. It is not uncommon for a child, at first, to make a big deal out of the new environment and advantages of living with the substitute parents, relative. It is quite common for a child to comment on such things and I remind the parents to expect such statements. I also prepare the child for the encounter and remind her that her parents might take offense or feel inadequate if she chooses to go on and on about her new situation and its advantages.

Although as the substitute parent you may have had little to do with the circumstances leading to the placement, you will need to know how to handle such feelings in an emotionally charged atmosphere and relationships that are new, unusual, and often strained.

It helps to start with the concept that the parents truly want their child to do well in substitute care. That has been my overwhelming impression of the parents I have encountered. There are exceptions to this rule and those parents may work diligently to sabotage the placement and undermine Sarah's success, as well as your efforts. Those exceptions aside, most of the disgruntled parents I have dealt with became disgruntled and problematic due primarily to how they were treated by either the authority or substitute parents involved.

Sarah may share some of the same feelings of her parents. No doubt there is some confusion and being "OK" with being away from her family might be perceived by her as being disloyal. Sarah's unhappiness or oppositional behavior might be more pronounced prior to and immediately after contacts with her family or non-custodial parent. The anticipated contact and actual contact serves as harsh reminders of her and their loss. It is also possible she is receiving instruction and "coaching" from the disgruntled party.

Following a visit or contact a typical complaint of the substitute parent is, "Sarah isn't herself after a visit," or "Sarah is so quiet and won't talk after she calls her Dad." Each visit and contact brings forth the issues of separation and loss and the younger the child, the more pronounced their reaction might be.

As the substitute parent there are things you can do to help alleviate some of the stress, pain, and conflict family visits can generate.

Create a cooperative atmosphere, and encourage open communication.

You will need to engender an immediate atmosphere of cooperation and reassure Sarah that her "real" family matters, and that their involvement will be welcomed.

She will need your encouragement to openly discuss her feelings about her family and the situation without her feeling disloyal or ungrateful to either them or you. This starts immediately upon her joining your family and can be addressed through little matters, such as how she wants to address you and other members of your family. These initial talks convey a message to Sarah that sets the tone for later discussions on more consequential matters.

Sarah will need this encouragement to talk throughout her time in your family. As she becomes more familiar and comfortable within her new family she may have internal conflicts over her "disloyalty" to her "real" family, friends, school, and neighborhood that can place her in a difficult emotional bind.

Open and honest communication with you serving as the active listener will provide the most help to her in dealing with the loyalty issue, as well as other matters pertaining to her "real" family.

RESPECT – that is what she needs from you...

With due apology to Aretha Franklin, her song hits the bulls eye on Sarah, her family, and how you need to act.

It is vital that you express a respectful manner towards the "real" family. Do not speak in a negative or derogatory manner about her family. You may have good cause to be upset and angry, often about how the family has treated Sarah, but keep those thoughts to yourself. If Sarah speaks in a negative or derogatory manner about her family, be careful not to "step on her lines," let her talk, without your agreement or disagreement, reflecting the feelings as hers, not yours. You will, no doubt, learn how to bite your tongue and withhold judgment throughout this process. If you can do so, Sarah will come to her own conclusions and you have maintained that respectful stance as to her and her family.

Be careful in this process as Sarah may express your opinion and in a moment of enthusiasm or joy, you jump in and declare your happiness that she has come to the "right" decision or opinion, only to watch this opinion change in front of your eyes simply because you endorsed it or she has reconsidered. Her opinions and decisions about her family need to be hers, without your endorsement or unsolicited advice.

If Sarah would ask for your input, again be careful and be sure she does want to hear what you have to say. If so, say as little as possible and give her time to digest and respond. With time and a cautionary response, your relationship has a better chance of improving. Sarah may indeed move towards a more realistic perception of her family due to your listening, discussing, reflecting, and shaping without adverse repercussions to your relationship. Family matters, regardless of how bad the family may appear, are extremely volatile issues and need more cautionary handling than any other situation.

This does not mean you should act in an uncaring or uninvolved manner. It is OK and called for to ask questions so she can think further and more in depth which may assist her in arriving at a workable decision or opinion.

I have dealt with this routinely since the beginning of my career. In residential care the major disappointment children have is over parents not coming for scheduled visitations.

A typical scenario is for Sarah to become more anxious as the visitation time draws near. If the parents have a history of not showing up, the anxiety, of course, increases, and often Sarah will declare, "Screw it, I ain't going."

What is the response called for? Think "time" again, give her a little time, a minute to reconsider, then approach in this or a similar fashion.

"Sarah, it sounds like you have been disappointed and are feeling that way again. I'm sure that is very frustrating, not knowing if they will show up. Give yourself a few minutes to think about it. We could ride over together to see if they are at the meeting place. If so, great! If not maybe you and I could handle a few of those errands we need to take care of, shopping, picking up something to eat or whatever. Do you want to call or have me call to see if they are coming or are already there?"

These statements are neither critical of Sarah or her parents nor do they ignore or endorse her feelings. It reflects her feelings, gives her time for reconsideration, and offers positive alternatives. You are offering concrete support and providing a diversion from the source of her frustration and pain. The message also indicates you like spending time with Sarah. This is important as the people who she feels should want to spend time with her have not met this need, and may have her feeling "unworthy" of their attention. Your behavior can directly refute this feeling, not by words of consolation, but action on your part.

HONOR PRIVACY

When it is necessary to discuss anything that has to do with Sarah and her family, make it a private conversation. Be very careful who you talk to and with about Sarah as confidentiality is essential to good parenting and building a decent relationship. There are very few people who need to hear what you have to say, and those you can openly talk with should also value confidentiality and privacy. There will be times and occasions when you will need to vent, that is expected, just be aware of where you are venting and to whom.

When Sarah uses the phone to call family members, give her space and ample time so she can converse in private and maybe do a little venting of her own. Set your phone time limits prior to making the call as an interruption can lead to unnecessary hard feelings and possible escalation on both ends of the phone line.

The same holds true for visitations. Do not interrupt or butt in; this is their time with their child and her time with them. The exception to this rule would be if Sarah requests you to check in on her during the visits or you have been required to do so due to safety issues. When safety issues enter into the picture, be sure you have a full understanding of what the concerns are and with whom. You do not have to be the "monitor" and I would strongly advise against playing this role as it does not enhance your relationship with the child or the family. If safety issues are in play, get the visits set up in a public place or under the auspices of an agency or professional. Don't try to be the hero; don't expose the child or yourself to a danger. Get to know all of the visitation parties prior to hosting a family visit in your own home or in a private area where help is not available.

As the substitute parent (or custodial parent) you have Sarah for most of the time, probably 90% or more if in foster or relative care. Be respectful of the 10% time afforded her "real" family or non-custodial parent.

If visits are to be held in your home or a public place, try to make the visitation environment as family friendly as possible. Can these visits be held in their home or neighborhood? Can they be arranged so that Sarah can have her family involved in church and school functions? Can they attend open houses, school conferences, and ball games? What about family birthdays and holidays? Can you schedule your special times around theirs? Can you take on the major burden of transportation, or at least assist? Can you accommodate extra relatives, siblings, and pets?

All of these questions involve preparation of the child and family for a successful interaction. Open communication with Sarah and her family should result in getting their input on some of the questions. Such input may provide you with a better idea as to how to proceed, prepare, and plan. It also portrays you as a helpful cooperative non-threatening adult who has consideration for their feelings and needs. You very well may not be able to accommodate all of their ideas, but just a little flexibility can make a positive impact.

One young man I worked with, Carlos, was very concerned as to his mother getting to and from our agency for visits. She had to ride the city bus then walk across campus and money was very tight. Her interest in Carlos and their relationship was good and above the norm. When Carlos and I discussed the above I agreed to provide transportation home if she showed the desire and ability to get to the visits as scheduled and on time. Both he and his mother agreed to this and were grateful for the accommodation. She never failed or missed a scheduled visit following this accord.

Transitions are always difficult for children. This is especially true at the end of the visitation times. Saying goodbye again can be heart wrenching and painful, bringing up all of the other goodbyes and losses incurred. Allow for time in saying goodbye, allow the child time and space to re-enter your world. Preparation and clear communication goes a long way, with both Sarah and her parents, in this transition period.

Maintaining respect and honoring privacy also includes your refraining from being "nosey" and/or interrogating Sarah following the visits. This can be difficult to do as we all want to know how these visits went so we can help the child and/or correct faulty information received. Back off, give time and space, keep your questions simple and supportive, "Hey Sarah, how did the visit go?"

If she seems emotionally upset or troubled, acknowledge such but keep your questions simple, supportive, and non-judgmental, "Gee Sarah, are you alright? Anything I can help you with?" This affords her the opportunity to talk if she so desires or remain quiet, as the question was not directive in nature or requires much of a response. Silence is fine; let it be, then follow up a little later with support, "Hey, I am here if and when you want to talk." Check back with her later, but avoid nagging.

If and when she chooses to discuss the visit or her feelings and concerns, listen, listen, and listen, utilizing reflective responses and all of the active listening skills. Be cautious in offering advice, but acknowledge her courage and credit for talking.

REMEMBER, WHEN DEALING WITH SARAH'S "REAL" FAMILY AND VISITS:

Keep your commitments.

Be punctual.

Stick to the schedule. Be supportive. Prepare the child. Don't cancel.

"Smooth" the transitions.

"Those who educate children well are more to be honored than they who produce them; for these only gave them life, those the art of living well."
-Aristotle

Chapter 11

What do I do when Sarah says she has a "secret?"

"Like the butterfly
I have the strength and the hope
to believe in time,
I will emerge from my cocoon,
Transformed."
-Kristi A. Dyer

As Brad walked by Kenny's room one warm spring night, he noticed Kenny in bed with all of his covers pulled up to his face.

Brad, having worked with the 10 year old Kenny for over six months found this behavior to be very unusual and inquired as to if he was feeling poorly.

Kenny responded "No," but then asked Brad who was working tonight after Brad left. Kenny was concerned as to who would be on his dorm later after lights were out. This, too, was an unusual comment by Kenny and Brad asked why he wanted to know.

Kenny was reluctant to clarify but then asked Brad if all of the doors and windows were locked and checked. Brad was again puzzled by this question but assured Kenny everything was locked and would again be checked prior to his leaving work later. He also told the troubled young man that Vernon would be the third shift youth care worker and would be on duty all night.

After Brad made his rounds checking on residents, doors, and windows, he stopped by Kenny's room to see if he was asleep. He found Kenny awake and again asked if he was feeling alright. Kenny said he was feeling fine and then Brad asked why Kenny was concerned tonight about windows, doors, and staff. He also noted to Kenny that he seemed trouble and preoccupied tonight.

As they talked, Kenny slowly revealed that he had seen someone on our campus earlier this evening.

Brad, who was aware of Kenny's history, (the reported as well as the suspected) inquired further as to who he had seen earlier that day. Kenny informed him it was a friend of his father who at one time had spent considerable time around Kenny and his two sisters. Both of the girls had reported being molested by a "family friend," and we had thought that Kenny had been a victim although he would not confirm this suspicion. Kenny, in counseling, in fact had been adamant that nothing had happened to him.

Brad asked Kenny if he liked this friend and he replied, "No, I don't." Brad then inquired if he was afraid of this man, and he responded, "Yes, a little."

Brad then assured Kenny he would remain on the dorm, check all the doors, and windows, talk with Vernon when he arrived, and check on him again before leaving. This seemed to provide some comfort for him but he continued to toss and turn, get in and out of bed, and check on Brad's whereabouts.

After an hour of such behavior, Brad sat down at the foot of his bed and inquired, "Kenny what's going on?"

Kenny with tears asked Brad if he could keep a secret. Brad assured him he would listen to anything Kenny had to say but could not promise to keep secrets that might lead to him or someone else being hurt.

Kenny, using his own words and struggling with his emotions, was able to tell Brad that the man he had seen on campus was a friend of his dad's and also the man who had molested his sisters, "and did some bad stuff to me."

Kenny was very upset and Brad assured him he was safe in our facility. Kenny had thought this fellow was still incarcerated for the molest charges and was fearful he was looking for him or his sisters.

At this point Brad felt I needed to be contacted but wanted to get Kenny's agreement and informed Kenny he thought it a good time to call me. Kenny consented to this phone call, although the idea was not for him to discuss the situation with me.

Brad called me at home, informing me he thought Kenny was not only fearful but in the right frame of mind to talk about those issues we had suspected.

I did come on campus and Brad sat through most of my subsequent discussion with Kenny as he felt "safer" with Brad present.

Sure enough, Kenny was ready to talk and admitted this person was indeed the man who had molested him, too.

From our conversation that night we were able to make significant progress in his overall treatment and the fellow in question was arrested, charged with the other molest, and again incarcerated.   .

None of the above would have happened had it not been for Brad being aware and in tune to this young man. He had worked diligently to build relationships with the youngsters on his dorm and such work had paid a tremendous dividend for Kenny, his sisters, and other possible victims.

This sharing of a confidence led to Kenny truly opening up in therapy, with his parents, and sisters and subsequently he and his sisters were placed with their mother, although the plan had been to return all three home to their father.

There were two heroes in this encounter, Kenny for sharing his secret, and Brad for being available and handling this delicate situation with great care and sensitivity without losing sight of his overall responsibility, that is, the long term well-being of the child.

"Dare to reach out your hand into the darkness, to pull another hand into the light"
-Norman B. Rice

Let's be candid with ourselves. Many of us were attracted to this type of profession or involvement with such children as Kenny as we want to help; we want to be someone a child can turn to in his time of need and to trust. We want to be the person a child seeks for guidance and advice, the adult who can build a relationship where a child will approach you with a "secret." It is a heady feeling and it affirms in our minds that we are fulfilling our role as a helper.

But please be cautious, there is awesome responsibility that comes with this role. Take your time as you are entering a very emotional laden minefield for this child.

When Sarah approaches you with a "secret" a good place to start is to let her know you appreciate her seeing you as someone she can talk with in confidence.

Be sure she has your full attention; body language, eye contact, all things that need to be congruent and relay a message of "I am listening."

In Kenny's situation Brad not only listened, he first recognized something was not quite right. Brad saw Kenny in bed, with the covers pulled up to his chin, and recognized this as being very different for Kenny.

Coach Bob Knight was once asked what made the difference between a good basketball player and a great basketball player. His response, to paraphrase, was the difference between being good and great is the ability to not only see, but to recognize; to not only hear, but to listen.

Brad moved from good response to great response, with Kenny, by following the above maxim.

His relationship with Kenny as well as his history directly impacted his mode of inquiry. This will be true in your interactions as well.

Often a child's demeanor when initiating this discussion will give you an idea of the import. You can also give Sarah a couple of brief examples of secrets... those you can keep which are harmless and those you must share to protect everyone.

It is very interesting as to who, when, why, and where a child divulges a secret. The big bombshells seem, in my experience, to come when least expected.

REGARDLESS of your belief as to the VERACITY of the report... LISTEN CAREFULLY WITH ALL DUE RESPECT. Children have a way of "floating out" a story close to their own, to see how it goes over or if it goes over, much like a trial balloon.

Your initial response will either allow the child to open up or convince the child he is better off keeping his mouth shut.

Does Sarah tell you a lot of secrets? Who do those secrets involve? What is the nature or magnitude of the secrets she has shared in the past? Has she been generally reliable in what she discloses?

Start your inquiry with a general non-threatening question such as, "How big a secret is this?" or "Who does this involve?" or "How important is this secret to you or others?"

It is important for Sarah to know she can confide in you but that some things cannot be kept secret all of the time; whereas some secrets are fun to keep and cause no harm. Provide examples of both that will give her a sense of what kinds of secrets are safe and unsafe to keep.

Do not belittle what she tells you, regardless of the importance to you. Be careful not to minimize nor maximize her message. If it is important enough to her that it is a secret she wishes to share... it is important enough to warrant your full attention and helpful response.

"Nothing that grieves us can be called little: by the eternal laws of proportion a child's loss of a doll and a king's loss of a crown are events of the same size."
-Mark Twain

When I get a sense that the secret is serious, or it is the first time the child has chosen to share a secret with me, I typically respond in the following fashion:

"Sarah, I am pleased you want to share a secret with me, and I am proud you are willing to talk. But some secrets can cause us harm. I really want to hear what you have to say but if this secret could hurt you or others I cannot keep it a complete secret."

This offers her an opportunity to respond as she chooses, knowing the consequences and likelihood of your response to the information shared. It encourages her to open up and provides parameters for your subsequent behavior.

We cannot allow ourselves to be a party to secrets or confidences that jeopardize the health, safety, or welfare of others. Brad was able to get this message across to Kenny in a manner that encouraged him to share.

It is a wonderful thing when a child chooses to trust us and disclose, but we cannot fall into the trap of being a "secret keeper buddy" when we are charged with being in the parental and protector role.

As to Brad, he went on to a very successful career as a child therapist eventually earning a master's degree in social work.

As to Kenny, a year or so after his discharge and placement with his mother I received a note from her with a small Angel pin, thanking me for being the guardian angel for her children during their time of placement. Unfortunately Brad had left our program and I was unable to give him the pin as he was truly the guardian angel for Kenny.

As to the "friend/molester", we later discovered he was living with Kenny's dad when he was seen walking across our campus, although he had no idea the children were in placement. Adding to this irony was that I had known this "friend" when he and his brothers were younger, having served as the child protective services caseworker for his youngest brother. All of the brothers, including him, had been molested by a "friend" of their mothers.

I have wondered what might have been his course in life if he, too, had confided early to a Brad, a Brad who saw, and recognized, heard and listened, and then acted in his best interests.

Chapter 12

What do I do when I think Sarah needs professional help?

"What the caterpillar calls the end of the world, the master calls the butterfly." -Richard Bach

A number of children going through the trauma of separation, loss, grief, and disruption will require and/or be required to engage in a therapeutic relationship with a professional therapist, counselor, psychologist, or psychiatrist.

Although I believe you, as the "substitute" parent, have the potential to be the most therapeutic influence in a child's life, seeing a clinician can be very helpful.

If you have not been involved in this process, and if Sarah has not been involved in this process, there are some things that need to be done so you structure this interaction to be positive and helpful.

If there is a case manager involved, that person would be responsible for setting up the appointments and notifying parents, however, if not, these obligations could fall on your shoulders. Sarah may come to your care already seeing a therapist and it will be your responsibility to keep those appointments.

Regardless... you need to acquaint yourself with the professional involved as well as the treatment goals and services offered.

If Sarah is not involved and you feel she could benefit from such services, I would recommend you talk it over with her family members that are involved in her life and get their input. As in any other conversation with Sarah, I recommend you be direct and attempt to answer any questions posed by her or her family. If a question involves information you are unsure of or don't know, make a note so you can bring this up when you meet with the therapist.

Your introduction to the topic should include why you think this might be of assistance for Sarah, her family, and you. Also discuss what can be expected.

If the appointment is her first, let her know what you know about the service as well as general information on the professional. Sharing such information may alleviate anxiety and dispel false assumptions or perceptions.

When I have had such discussions, some of the comments made by Sarah/Johnny are, "Do you think I'm crazy?" or "I'm not crazy, I don't need to see a shrink!" Generally their view of professional help is quite different from ours, and we need to help get them through another difficult transition. We also need to directly respond to those comments and acknowledge that seeing a professional is not a sign of "craziness" or abnormality, and if given the chance such a person might be of major assistance.

You want Sarah to know as much as possible as to what she is getting into prior to the first meeting.

When you start the process of seeking professional assistance, the first question needing consideration is, "What does Sarah need from a professional assistant?" The second question should be, "What do I need from our professional assistant?"

I utilize the term professional assistant as this is how such should be viewed, not as experts or "fixers," but as people with experience, skills, and knowledge to hopefully help Sarah help herself, and help you be more successful in your substitute parental role.

Having served as a "professional assistant" for 35 plus years, I have great respect and regard for others in this line of work. However, I have an even higher regard and esteem for those of you in the parental and direct child care role, as you may be the primary change agent in that child's life. In this primary change agent role, all of the rest of us involved serve in secondary roles and it is essential that you view us as adjuncts and assistants, as the hard work will be done by Sarah and you.

As assistants we can help direct, teach, guide, consult, build skills, listen, prescribe and refer... but the nuts and bolts, the day in and day out efforts are yours and hers.

When seeking a professional assistant, be a careful selector or buyer of such services. If you can take the perspective of a "buyer" of services you may be in a better position to ask the necessary questions. I fear all too often people are uncomfortable in the "buyer" role and rely upon others to make such referrals and decisions. This may come from being unsure, naïve, or the feeling that you lack the necessary knowledge to get Sarah to the right person.

Getting the opinions of others is always a good idea, including Sarah's, as she may have had other experiences that will impact her progress with a new person. Family, friends, clergy, and teachers can serve to steer you in the right direction or at least keep from going in the wrong way.

Over the years I have made countless such referrals, but I always provide at least three names requesting they do the research, weigh, and consider before engaging the doctor, therapist, and/or psychiatrist. Sarah and you will have to live with the final choice made so it needs to be primarily hers and yours.

So, with the above caveats stated, what do you look for when seeking professional help?

Obviously you want someone with education, experience, and expertise. Your child's trauma history is important to know and consider. If Sarah has been a victim of sexual abuse, you want to engage a practitioner with experience in working with sexual abuse victims and families. You would not send Sarah to a podiatrist for asthma, and the same holds true in this case.

It is also important to know if the practitioner is comfortable working with people under age 18. In my experience I have known a number of good therapists, but quite a few of them, for various reasons, had no desire to work with kids who are trauma victims. Please don't waste Sarah and your time working with someone who does not want to work with you.

Some questions to consider as you go about this task…

Do you feel comfortable with this person?

Do you seem to understand each other? This does not necessarily imply you are in agreement but at least you can communicate openly, in language and terminology you both understand. Far too many people I have known have left therapy and treatment as they could not understand the language or felt comfortable to openly discuss issues with the therapist.

Does this person demonstrate, in your preliminary discussion, an understanding of Sarah's developmental stage and current level of functioning?

Does this person emphasize her strengths, total environment, skill building, and your importance in the entire treatment process?

Is this person open and candid as to his approach, methods, philosophy, or "school of thought" in regards to treatment? Hopefully the professional you choose will utilize evidence based treatment practices. In your opinion do the above "fit" with the needs of Sarah and your family?

Does this person seem to be someone with whom Sarah can and will communicate? Initial reluctance on Sarah's part is to be expected, but you need to get a feel for whether with a little time the therapist will be able to engage Sarah.

Is the treatment offered goal oriented, evidence based, and focused on realistic benchmarks and parameters? A good indicator of such is the professional who helps the child, the family, and you formulate realistic goals that can be successfully met with due diligence by all parties.

Does this person appear to be one who will hold all parties accountable in treatment? Success and progress in treatment is hard work and a good professional should assign homework for all involved, and not simply rely upon the work getting done in the scheduled sessions.

Does this person honor Sarah's, her family's, and your other commitments? Mary Pipher, a professional therapist in her book, *The Shelter of Each Other*, addresses this issue. She writes, "A good rule of thumb is that life is more important than therapy. Friends, family, work, school, vacations, ballgames, are all more important than therapy, because the goal of therapy is to get them into healthy normal activity."

Be skeptical of professionals who...

are eager to diagnose

approach Sarah and/or your family as "dysfunctional" or "abnormal"

want to take control of the treatment process

serve more as a "guru" than a therapist

over utilize or depend upon the reports and opinions of others spend the majority of the time advising and instructing

perceive the treatment time as being the most important activity in Sarah's life

I would recommend, if at all possible, a pre-session meeting with the professional you are planning to engage. This gives you the opportunity to ask questions and discuss concerns without the child present, or left sitting in the lobby wondering what you are telling the therapist. It also sends a very strong message to the therapist that you will be an active participant in the treatment process.

Such a prep session provides you information you can share with Sarah, and her family, that may ease her anxiety.

Prior to the actual introduction and session you can give her an idea of what and who to expect. Although Sarah may have been seen by a number of professionals in the past, it will help to do this preparation. Let her know that you will start the session or appointment with her then bow out when asked or the time seems appropriate to do so.

With apologies to Dr. Seuss, at the start the WHO will be more critical than the WHAT. Sarah will connect or disconnect quicker with the WHO, than the WHAT. If the WHO can engage her THEY will get to the WHAT in good time.

All of this sends a message to both the child and therapist, "I am involved;" and "I want this to be successful;" and "I care."

Of course it is important for Sarah to have her own private time with the professional and to understand the confidentiality of the session or meeting. She needs to feel free to express herself in her own way about whatever the issue or concern may be. This could include feelings, gripes, opinions, and thoughts about you and the care you are providing.

Allowing and honoring this process signals trust, respect, and confidence in her, yourself and the therapist.

I usually do a few minutes of warm up time with the child and therapist then bow out with, "Hey, I think you can talk with Dr._____ on your own quite well. I'll wait in the lobby, if you have questions or need me to come back in, just let me know"

Practice and such warm ups are essential for Sarah, especially if this is the first meeting or experience. Doing so with her also teaches a valuable lesson, practice helps us when we face new, unpleasant, and/or difficult tasks.

One set of grandparents I worked with missed the boat on this strategy. It was their view that the therapy was for their grandson, and they would drop him off and either sit in their car or leave until the session was concluded. He was of the age where he could enter the office and check in without help. But as he told me later, he felt a lack of support and involvement by his grandparents, as if they were saying, "Here you are, go get fixed, and come out better." In reality, his grandparents were very caring, but were unsure what their role in the treatment process should or could be.

If you are an experienced professional care giver, it is also easy to assume too much when we have worked over and over with children presenting very similar issues. Children with a history of placement and treatment are often perceived as "treatment savvy," they are experienced and know what to say and when to say it.

Be cautious as children are not as savvy as we tend to give them credit. Even those children with lengthy histories of care and treatment should be afforded the same courtesy and preparation as a child on his first visit to a counselor or doctor.

A recent experience with a youngster served to remind me of this caveat. Jeff, a 15 year old in care, and I were on the way to see a new psychiatrist, Dr. _____. I could sense from Jeff's comments that he was a little anxious. As I asked a few more probing questions Jeff blurted out, "Will this doctor give me a shot? I hate shots!"

I was surprised by this remark as I thought, with Jeff's history and experience he knew full well what would take place in a psychiatrist's office. After a quick assurance that this particular doctor was not one who administered shots, I carefully went over what he could expect during this visit.

While I had been thinking Jeff to doctor = help for Jeff, Jeff had been thinking, Jeff to doctor = shots and pain for Jeff. Obviously we were not on the same page and the failure to communicate was due to my taking his thinking for granted.

It is easy to fall into this pattern with children, believing Jeff's thinking and understanding were the same as mine.

In this particular case no true harm was done, but how often does this take place between a child and parent and at what costs?

So what do you do when you disagree with the professional's recommendation? What if medication is recommended for Sarah?

As the primary caretaker, especially as a step, foster, or grandparent, ask the questions that are on your mind. Feel free to advocate for the child and represent Sarah's interests and feelings. If you are aware of certain feelings or ideas she has, share those with the professional prior to the first meeting. If you know Sarah has been on medication before and did not respond well, tell the therapist or doctor this at the start, and you may avoid some conflicts.

Do not be intimidated by your professional assistant(s). Feel free to disagree, be skeptical, and voice your opinion.

If you don't understand something, it is a safe bet Sarah does not understand either.

Ask questions! The only stupid question is the one you don't ask! Remember you are the one living with Sarah. She and you have the most to lose or gain, and any decent professional will appreciate your concern, effort, and input.

As to the issue of medications, generally it has been my experience that medications can be a viable tool in the treatment of some children and adolescents. So much depends upon the age of the child as well as the problem being experienced, behavior exhibited, degree and severity of the behavior, and, of course, the medication prescribed. You need to closely monitor the effects on Sarah and engage her in the process of self-reporting effects. Also enlist the support of others in the family as well as teachers and adults who have close contact with Sarah, this should include members of her "real" family if involved.

As to the age of the child you need to be aware that psychotropic medications are basically "adult" medications. These medications were formulated, tested, and approved for adults under the supervision of licensed practitioners.

As in anything else, buyer beware, user beware, question authority, and closely monitor impact as well as side effects.

Please do not view medications as a "magic bullet" or mystery cure that can be utilized alone as a means of modifying the child's behavior or emotions. However, a therapeutic dose administered by a licensed practitioner in conjunction with and as part of a plan of treatment can be beneficial in many cases. Sarah may, with the use of medication, improve self-control, focus, attention, and alleviate some of the symptoms.

Medicating children without an overall treatment plan is, in my opinion, unethical and will be proven ineffective in time.

Know your doctor, utilize only those fully trained to administer and prescribe. There are more and more general practitioners prescribing such medications today than before due primarily to, at least in our area, a shortage of child psychiatrists and their overwhelming case loads. Most of the general practitioners have been great and a "Godsend," when a psychiatric consult could not be arranged in a timely manner. However, if you can get in with a child psychiatrist or clinical practitioner do so as they have the education and expertise.

Please be sure to check with Sarah as to her feelings about medication. Some of the children I have worked with had medications prescribed and when we left the doctor's office they informed me, "That doesn't work for me," or "I'm allergic to that med." Then there have been a few adolescents who have simply stated, "I won't take the medication." If there is a refusal, explore why and honor that request, at least for the time being, and see how the child responds.

A few years back a very wise Grandma utilized me in such a role. I was her fourteen year old grandson's Sunday school teacher. She stopped me one day after church services to get my "educated opinion" on Todd and what my observations had been. He seemed to me, and I reported such, to be a normally developed eighth grade male adolescent, no different than most of the young men I had in class over the years. Grandma seemed relieved with this response and when I inquired about her concerns she informed me that Todd's mother felt he was "hyperactive" and she had started him on medication for ADHD a few years previously. Grandma at no time felt he was in need of such and was concerned about the long term effects of the medication.

I advised Grandma that my observations of Todd were limited, but he had not impressed me as "hyper." I quickly added that maybe he did not appear "hyper" to me as he was on the medication. I also stated that his behavior in class had been very good but could have something to do with the structure, expectations, peer group, and his interest. I encouraged her to seek the opinion and input of others then approach her daughter and discuss her concerns.

Grandma later reported to me that she did as I had suggested, gathered the information, and then did sit down with both parents. They agreed to bring Todd into the discussion and found out he did not like taking the medication and felt he was of the age that he should at least be given the opportunity to try life without the medication. With the direction and guidance of the prescribing physician, Todd began a gradual reduction of the medication. With this reduction Todd assumed more responsibility for his behavior as he wanted to prove to all he could handle himself med free.

Todd's medication over a few months were gradually decreased and discontinued.

Not all cases are as successful nor are all grandmas as observant, caring and courageous as Todd's. But her actions on his behalf led others to provide realistic feedback to the parents and doctor who then had reason to reconsider and adjust the treatment accordingly.

As the adult in the substitute role it is a good idea to check in, as this grandma did, with other adults involved with the child to get their perceptions. As mentioned before, teachers, friends, coaches, and babysitters see Sarah in different settings than you. Their interactions are taking place in different social environments and their input may prove very valuable, so listen carefully and not simply to confirm your own opinion.

It is important that you gather facts, not just opinions. Invest in a PDR, Physician's Desk Reference, it gives great information and is not a slick "promotional" pamphlet of the drug manufacturer. You can be a much more effective advocate when you are informed.

It has been my good fortune to have worked with a large number of highly qualified and dedicated psychiatrists and practitioners. Although we have not always seen eye to eye, my concerns have been listened to and given due consideration.

Sarah and many of her peers will need help above and beyond what you, or I, can provide. Your involvement and oversight of the treatment will best assure she gets the help she needs from the best possible professional you engage.

"To ease another's heartache is to forget one's own."
-Abraham Lincoln

SUMMARY

"Sweet freedom whispered in my ear,
You're a Butterfly
And Butterflies are free to fly
Fly away, high away, bye bye."
Someone Saved My Life Tonight, Elton John/Bernie Taupin

Maybe you won't actually save someone's life, but I am convinced your efforts can free a butterfly or two.

It is my sincere wish and fervent hope that what you have gleaned from this book has been of help and will continue to serve you in your wonderful quest to be the "best" parent you can be to "your" child.

If this book has helped, I first and foremost want to thank the leading characters, those beautiful butterflies who sometimes screamed, sometimes laughed, sometimes cursed, sometimes prayed, sometimes cried, sometimes smiled… the Hakeem's, Seth's, Sharon's, and Karen's that taught me more than I ever taught them as I watched them learn to fly. It was an honor to be a part of your lives.

In the introduction I stated I would address the question as to "What is wrong with the children today?"

I am asked that same question almost daily by parents, teachers, police, and concerned individuals. These people want to know what is going on with kids, why do they behave the way they do… breaking laws, using drugs, failing in school, disrespecting authorities, and demonstrating little regard for society's norms.

My response is basically this: children do show respect for societal norms, in fact their behavior is far too often a direct reflection of what they see in their homes, communities, and society in general.

Children are no different today than they were 20, 40, or 400 years ago, IF you consider the families, communities, and societies in which they live.

"Children of today are tyrants. They contradict their parents, gobble their food, and tyrannize their teachers."
-Socrates 469 BC

Are children today more violent, unstable, emotional, selfish, sexualized, irresponsible, irreverent, hedonistic, materialistic... probably so.

However, look at our families and at the environments that produce and stimulate our children and you will see more violence, instability, emotionality, selfishness, sexuality, irresponsibility, irreverence, hedonism, and materialism.

I would suggest before we waste our time pointing fingers at our children we might want to first look at ourselves, our families, and our communities.

As to ourselves...do we model the behavior we want to see?

"Children need models rather than critics."
-Joseph Jonbert

"Don't worry that children never listen to you. Worry that they are always watching you."
-Robert Fulgham

Mr. Joubert and Mr. Fulgham may have hit the bull's eye with the above statements, as it would appear to me that our children today closely mirror our own performance. The more a child sees selfish behavior, the more selfish you can expect him to act.

As I have pointed out throughout this work, YOU are the most important person in your child's world, if you choose to be. Relationships are what counts, and a child is more likely to change his behavior based on a strong healthy relationship with an adult than any other factor.

As to our families, we bemoan not being the influence we should be to our children, but do we spend as much time working on this as we do complaining, do we spend as much time on our families as we do our profession? I am not throwing rocks as I, too, live in a glass house, but introspection is of primary importance before we look outward.

We bemoan all of the outside influences, friends, media, internet, music, movies, magazines, BUT what do we do to structure our youth's intake of such, to mediate such influences, to honestly talk about these things openly and honestly with our kids, and to provide them healthy alternatives?

"Let us put our minds together and see what life we can make for our children."
-Sitting Bull

The focus of this book has been on the parenting of children other than our own, and I don't want to get too far from that topic.

However, after we look at ourselves we need to look at our communities and ask, "How might we improve our community for our children and those children being parented by others?"

Every community has its problems and limits, especially finances. I have been proud of my home community, not because we are perfect; far from it (I am sure there are communities that surpass mine in this effort). However, private and public people and organizations, including government officials, strive to provide the best we can with our limited resources.

We do not always agree on What needs to be done for Whom and with What resources… but we make a concerted effort to do the best we can for our youth who we all say are the most valuable resource of a community. We know as adults that we cannot solve all of the world's problems, but I believe the place to start is within our immediate families, neighborhoods, and communities. To paraphrase an old saying, "We can either curse the dark or start lighting candles where we live."

I cannot remember who said this but I once read a comment that struck me as profound. The comment was that if you want to find out what a community values, look at what they build… is it churches, community centers, parks, health clinics, schools, hospitals or is it sports arenas, banks, entertainment areas, and shopping malls. The gist of this message is if you want to know what a community values, find out where its treasures go, it will probably tell you where its heart is.

This is not to be a social commentary or political diatribe. I hope the following points stimulate your thoughts, give you cause to reflect, and possibly take action.

As Francis Bacon wrote years ago... *"Read not to contradict nor to believe, but to weigh and consider."*

How might we connect the child with one stable adult throughout his placement outside of the home?

How might we limit the number of placements for a child when he leaves his parental home?

How might we rethink the present rule of thumb; and in some states the law, that the "least restrictive placement" should be tried first?

Maybe we need to be a little more restrictive and evaluative of the child's needs when removed from his family, rather than focusing on the "restrictiveness" of the environment. It has been my experience that a child who is first evaluated and assessed has a better chance of being appropriately placed.

How might we improve utilization of our resources to prevent placements? How might we maximize prevention and decrease maintenance services? We presently spend $1000's on a child's therapy, medications, placements, when maybe a membership in the Y or Boy's Club might be a critical need.

I do not believe in throwing money at a problem thinking that will fix it. The point I am making however, is the more preventative measures we can provide and offer are going to be considerably less expensive than the cure. I have always been able to access the bigger bucks easier than I have been able to come up with the $100 needed for school clothes, books, fees, scout membership, etc.

How might we provide realistic "wrap around services," for our child before he needs placement? How might we provide realistic "follow up services" for the child after he leaves placement and returns to his family?

How might we teach the child what he needs to know to be productive in this world?

One of the areas that concerns me and is a "pet peeve," so to speak, is opportunities for a child to work. As stated previously, my father was a big believer in kids learning how to work early in life and how to earn something from their own labor. Years back there were a number of programs for adolescents that "taught" them how to work. Our children need to learn to be "owners" and workers, to be productive and it needs to start early with such programs as the old Neighborhood Youth Corps, where kids worked summer months in their communities doing various jobs, painting, street cleaning, and park recreation.

How might we better advocate for children's rights?

"The youth of our nation are the clearest mirror of our performance."
-Senator Robert F. Kennedy 1968

How might our churches better serve the children in their neighborhoods?

How might our schools better serve our students and what should our role be in supporting the educational system and its teachers in this endeavor? I know in my community our school system and personnel have worked diligently to meet the needs of our youth and families in many areas. But far too often when a problem comes up we expect the schools to handle it or unfairly criticize them for not immediately and adequately addressing and resolving whatever the issue is at hand.

The easiest job in the world is, in my opinion, to be a critic. It only requires an eye for looking out rather than healthy introspection, and a finger pointing at others rather than a helping hand held out. School systems are an easy and convenient target for such critics. What we all need, every agency and government entity, is constructive criticism offered with help and a willingness to commit one's own sweat, time, and resources in providing solutions—after all, they are all our kids.

How might our Courts become more "child and family" friendly?

Although we are fortunate to have an innovative and active Juvenile Court (and Judges) in our locale, I am in favor of Family Courts, more so than Juvenile Courts. Such courts could be geared to handling family and children issues, including divorce, delinquent, abuse and neglect cases. So many of the children I have worked with did not start having major problems until their nuclear family broke down, often due to divorce. The parents, who are already at odds, are left to decide what is in the best interest of the child, often without the child's best interest being considered. Some states and courts are moving towards "divorce mediation" services which give serious consideration to the children involved and their needs.

How might we revamp the system in place to prioritize delivery of services?

It has always seemed ironic to me that when I first started in this profession I was given the toughest cases. I had the least experience working with the most difficult families and children and given the least resources to do so. If I had started my professional career as an auto mechanic, I doubt I would have been handed a set of tools during my orientation and told to fix a damaged transmission. My guess is I would have started out changing oil and oil filters, learning as I go and receiving the resources I needed to do the expected job with serious evaluation of my effort and ability.

We do not do that in this profession and I think that holds true in most "helping/people service" professions. Let's get our most talented and experienced folks working with those children and families needing their expertise, not the rookies coming into the field.

I do not have all of the answers to the above and I am sure many others may pose more germane questions than the preceding.

I do believe, however, until we start to address these issues on a community basis we will continue to "short change" our children, who are supposed to be our most valuable resource.

"What's done to children they will do to society."
-Karl Menninger

No doubt there is much left to be done and the children yearning and deserving to be butterflies deserve our best efforts.

To those of you engaged in this wonderful effort you are in my thoughts and prayers and I wish to leave you with a prayer to consider that is much more eloquent than yours truly could write.

Dear Heavenly Father

Make me a better parent.

Teach me to understand my children, to listen patiently to what they have to say and to answer all of their questions kindly.

Keep me from interrupting them, talking back to them and contradicting them.

Make me as courteous to them as I would have them be to me.

Give me the courage to confess my sins against my children and ask their forgiveness when I know that I have done them wrong.

May I not vainly hurt the feelings of my children. Forbid that I should laugh at their mistakes or resort to shame and ridicule as punishment.

Let me not tempt my child to lie or steal. So guide me hour by hour that I might demonstrate by all I say and do that honesty produces happiness.

Reduce, I pray, the meanness in me. May I cease to nag: and when I am out of sorts help me, O Lord, to hold my tongue.

Blind me to the little errors of my children.

Help me grow up with my children to treat them as those of their age, but let me not expect of them the judgments and conventions of adults.

Allow me not to rob them of the opportunity to wait upon themselves, to think, to choose, to make decisions.

Forbid that I should ever punish them for my selfish satisfaction.

May I grant them all their wishes that are reasonable and have the courage always to withhold a privilege which I know will do them harm.

Make me fair and just, so considerate and companionable to my children that they will have a genuine esteem for me.

Fit to be loved and imitated by my children.

Amen.

(Author unknown)

Best wishes to you, yours, and "ours," and may our efforts serve to limit and mute the screams of the butterflies.

Gary C. Barnett

About the Author

Gary C. Barnett holds a BS degree from Middle Tennessee State University and an MA in Agency and Community Counseling from Indiana State University. Since 1973, Gary has worked with children and families, serving primarily as a counselor. Involvement includes Child Protective Services in Vanderburgh County, Indiana and as a Consultant for the State of Indiana Child Welfare Department. In 1988, Gary began his third association with Hillcrest Washington Youth Home in Evansville, Indiana, serving as the Program Administrator, Residential Services Director, and is the current Director of Treatment Services. Gary is also a "trained trainer" in Cornell University's Therapeutic Crisis Intervention, and a member of the I.A.R.C.C.A. state "Best Practices" task force on seclusions and restraints. He has been involved in his community, serving on the boards of both the Ark Crisis Prevention Nursery and Big Brothers/Big Sisters advisory board as well as coaching youth sports and teaching youth Sunday School at St. Paul's United Christian Church for over 20 years.

Suggested readings and bibliography

TO THE READER:

When I read I want to be

1)Informed,

2) Learn something,

3) Provoked to think, and

4) Entertained.

I hope you experience the first three in all of the below listed items, as for entertainment you will have to look elsewhere.

Cornell University Therapeutic Crisis Intervention Residential Child Care Project Family Life Development Center, college of Human Ecology, Seventh Edition 2010

Holden, M.J. and Levine-Powers, J. (1993) Therapeutic Crisis Intervention. The Journal of Emotional and Behavioral Problems, 2, 49-52.

Redl, F. (1959) Strategies and Techniques of the Life Space Interview, American Journal of Orthopsychiatry 29, 1-18.

Redl, F. (1966) When We Deal With Children, New York: Free Press

Growing Through Loss, Indianapolis Grief and Loss Consulting and Educational Services. P.K. Walker and M.L. Shaffer (2003)

Cates, J., Cummings,J., Recovering Our Children. Lincoln,NE. Writers Club Press (2003)

McVey-Nobel,M. Khemlani-Petal, S. Neziroglu. F. When Your Child Is Cutting. Oakland CA. New Harbinger Publications Inc. (2006)

Greenwald, R., Child Trauma Handbook. Boca Raton,FLA. Taylor and Francis Publishers. (2005)

Spinks, S., Adolescent Brains Are A Work in Progress. Frontline Publications. Nature, Volume 404 March 9, 2000

Winters, K., Arria, A. "Adolescent Brain Development and Drugs," The Prevention Researcher, Volume 18, November 2, 2011

Multiple Placements in Foster Care: Literature Review of Correlates and Predictors.

February 2004. Children and Family Research Center School of Social Work, University of Illinois.

Redding, T.E., Britner, P.A., and Fried, C., "Predictors of Placement Outcomes in Treatment," Journal of Child and Family Studies 9 (4) 425-447 (2000)

Cohen, J., Mannario, A., Deblinger, E. Treating Trauma and Traumatic Grief in Children and Adolescents. New York: The Guilford Press (2006) --- I recommend Part 1 Chapter 1 and Part 2 Chapter 2

Scowen, K. My Kind of Sad: What It's Like To Be Young and Depressed. Toronto: Annick Press LTF (2006)

Pipher, M. Reviving Ophelia; Saving the Selves of Adolescent . New York: Ballentine Books (1994)

Pipher, M., The Shelter of Each Other: Rebuilding Our Families. New York: G.P. Putnam Sons (1996)

Burke, R., Herron, R., and Barnes, B. Common Sense Parenting. Boys Town Press 3rd Edition

Wubbolding, R. Using Reality Therapy. New York: Harper and Row Publishers (1988)

McKay, M., Fanning, P., Prisoners of Belief. Oakland,CA: New Harbinger Publications Inc. (1991) -- -I recommend Chapters 1, 2, 3, and 4

Feindler, E., Ecton, R. Adolescent Anger Control: Cognitive Behavioral Techniques. New York: Pergamon Press (1986)

Mintz, S., Huck's Raft: A History of American Childhood. Cambridge,MA: Belknap (2004)

Horne, A., Sayger, T. Treating Conduct and Oppositional Defiant Disorders in Children. New York: Pergamon Press (1990)

Bertolino, B. Therapy with Troubled Teenagers. New York: John Wiley and Sons, Inc. (1999) --- I recommend Chapters 1, 2, and 3.

Phelan, T., Surviving Your Adolescents. Child Management Inc. Glen Ellyn: IL (1993)

Relationship and Communication Activities. P. Rizzo, TonerHealth Curriculum Activities Library, The Center for Applied Research in Education, W. Nyack: New York

(1993)

Gurian, M., The Wonder of Boys. Tarcher Putnam: New York (1997)

Steinberg, L., Levine, A., You and Your Adolescent. Harper Perennial: New York (1990)--- I recommend Chapters 1, 2, and 7.

Grossman, D., On Killing. Back Bay Books: New York (1996) -- - I recommend Section 1, Chapter 1 and Section 8, Chapters 1,2,3, and 4.

Anda, R., Felitti, V., The Adverse Childhood Experiences Study. Center for Disease Control and Prevention, (1998)

Felitti, V., The Relationship of Adverse Childhood Experiences to Adult Health: Turning Gold into Lead. San Diego, CA. (1998)

McKay, M., Fanning, P., Paleg, K. Landis, D. When Anger Hurst Your Kids: A Parent's Guide. Oakland, CA: New Harbinger Publications, Inc

Webb, N. Editor. Helping Bereaved Children: A Handbook for Practitioners. New York: The Guilford Press. (1993) --- I recommend Chapters 1, 2, 6, and 9

Braman, O.I., The Oppositional Child. Charlotte, N.C.,: KIDSRIGHT (1995)

Happy Reading!

CPSIA information can be obtained at www.ICGtesting.com
Printed in the USA
LVOW041950020113

314123LV00002B/50/P